T0339751

"*Coaching in Government* is a must read, especially for chief learning officers, learning practitioners, and program managers tasked with any organization's coaching initiatives. Readers will discover critical lessons learned and important steps to take in successfully establishing coaching programs, along with the importance of how coaching supports leadership development and further investments in learning."

Randy Bergquist, *former chair; Interagency Chief Learning Officer Council (2010–2016)*

"Governments are one of the major employers in just about any country. In the United States alone, Federal Government employs nearly 3 million civilian individuals. And as this book suggests, 'coaching provides a whole new paradigm – a coach approach to public service'. The benefits can be tremendous, sustainable, and far-reaching. This book offers a great insight into building coaching cultures within governmental agencies, all over the world."

Magdalena Nowicka Mook, *CEO; International Coaching Federation*

Coaching in Government

This book captures the story of how internal coaching was introduced—and has since evolved—in the U.S. Federal Government and provides coaches and government agency leaders with the skills and tools to help them implement their own successful coaching programs.

Written by leaders in the field, the book follows the stories of several pioneers who have implemented coaching programs in government, aiming to help coaches learn from their mistakes and gain from their wisdom. Filled with interviews, case studies, reflective questions, and how-to action points, each chapter accessibly highlights the successes and failures of each coach's journey so that professionals can incorporate these lessons in their own practice. Chapters take readers from the beginning considerations to contemplating the future of their programs, focusing on setting a vision, overcoming issues and challenges, leveraging predictors of success, making key decisions, building foundations for sustainability, and creating continuing education for sustainment of change. Accessible and relatable, these stories will help professionals learn from those that have come before them, helping them begin the groundswell of change effectively and proactively in their own programs.

This book is essential reading for coaches and government agency leaders, as well as for any public sector agency and any private sector organization that is interested in implementing coaching.

Theodora J. Fitzsimmons, PhD, PCC, PMP is a Leadership Development Expert, Leadership and Executive Coach, Coach Trainer, Coach Mentor, and Coaching Supervisor with decades of experience in the public and private sector.

Marykate Behan Dougherty, PCC, PMP is a Project Management Professional, Coach, Coach Trainer and Mentor, and Leadership Development Expert with over 30 years of private, government, nonprofit, and international experience.

Alan Lee Myers, MA, PCC, is a Leadership and Organizational Development Professional, Leadership/Executive Coach, Coach Trainer, Mentor Coach, Coaching Supervisor, and Public Health Specialist with over 35 years of government and nonprofit experience.

Coaching in Government

Stories and Tips for Coaching Professionals

THEODORA J. FITZSIMMONS
MARYKATE BEHAN DOUGHERTY
ALAN LEE MYERS

Routledge
Taylor & Francis Group

NEW YORK AND LONDON

Designed cover image: Getty Images

First published 2023
by Routledge
605 Third Avenue, New York, NY 10158

and by Routledge
4 Park Square, Milton Park, Abingdon, Oxon, OX14 4RN

Routledge is an imprint of the Taylor & Francis Group, an informa business

Library of Congress Cataloging-in-Publication Data
A catalog record for this title has been requested

ISBN: 978-1-032-11225-1 (hbk)
ISBN: 978-1-032-11223-7 (pbk)
ISBN: 978-1-003-21893-7 (ebk)

DOI: 10.4324/9781003218937

Typeset in Dante and Avenir
by codeMantra

We dedicate this book to all the current coaches, coaching program leaders, and the many champions of government programs. Thank you for your shared passion and continued service.

Contents

Author Biographies

Theodora J. Fitzsimmons, PhD, PMP, PCC, CCM, Accredited Coaching Supervisor
https://www.linkedin.com/in/theodorafitzsimmons/

Dr. Theodora Fitzsimmons is a Leadership and Professional Development Expert, Leadership and Executive Coach, Coach Trainer, Coach Mentor, and Coaching Supervisor with decades of experience in the public and private sector. She started her career in higher education administration and teaching and transferred to corporate training. After working as a Government Contractor for several years, she jumped into federal service, where she spearheaded initiatives and led training and leadership development teams. She created and led the award-winning DIA Coaching Program, with the goal of transforming the culture of the agency to one where more listening and open communication occurred. She is passionate about and provides coaching and team coaching to emerging leaders, teams, and senior executives in government because she believes that coaching enables these leaders to face the unprecedented challenges of today and the future in the workplace. She has served as a Lead Faculty Member and Coach Mentor in the Federal Internal Coach Training Program and has been instrumental in promoting and authoring the guidelines and policies that define coaching in the federal government. She owns a private coaching business, Coach Evolving, LLC, and is a partner of Radiance Partners, LLC, a coaching school.

Dr. T. Fitzsimmons completed her certification in professional coaching from the Institute of Professional Excellence in Coaching in 2014. She has also completed additional coach certifications from the NeuroLeadership Institute, Success Unlimited Network, and ACT Government Services. She is a Professional Certified Coach (PCC) through the International Coaching Federation (ICF). She earned her EMCC Global Team Coaching Individual Accreditation (ITCA) and professional designation at the practitioner level after completing the Global Team Coaching Institute training with Dr. David Clutterbuck in 2021. Her academic achievements include PhD in Training and Performance Improvement, Summa Cum Laude, Capella University, 2007; Master of Education in Curriculum and Instruction from the University of Maryland, College Park, Maryland, 1995; Bachelor of Arts in Business and Management, University of Maryland University College, 1984; Bachelor of Arts in Psychology, University of Maryland University College, 1982. She has also completed a diploma program from the Coach Supervision Academy in 2019 and is a coaching supervisor. Dr. T. Fitzsimmons nominated her agency for two International Awards and received the Excellence in Practice Award from the Association for Talent Development in 2018 and was a Finalist for the Prism Award from the International Coaching Federation in 2019.

Marykate Behan Dougherty, PCC, PMP

www.linkedin.com/in/marykate-behan-dougherty-pmp-pcc

Marykate Behan Dougherty is a Professional Certified Coach (PCC) through the International Coaching Federation (ICF) and a Project Management Professional (PMP) through the Project Management Institute with over 30 years of demonstrated competence and outstanding productivity as a Consultant, Program Manager, Project Leader, and Director. She has completed projects in North America, the Middle East, Asia, Africa, and the former Soviet Union. Along with her one-on-one coaching, Marykate is known for creating and presenting a wide assortment of unique experiential workshops and group coaching classes focused on personal transformation and sustainable change. She has designed, implemented, and managed ongoing programs for private, nonprofit, and government entities including NASA, the Government Accountability Office, and the Department of the Treasury.

M. Dougherty completed her certification in professional coaching from the Institute of Professional Excellence in Coaching in 2012. She is an Arbinger Trained Facilitator, Situational Leadership Trained Facilitator, Myers-Briggs Type Indicator Qualified User, Strength Deployment Inventory Qualified User, DiSC Practitioner, Energy Leadership Index Master Practitioner, and Social & Emotional Intelligence Profile Certified User. She completed a Master's Certificate in Project Management at The George Washington University. In addition, she has a Master of Arts in Education and Human Development from The George Washington University and a Bachelor of Science in Business Administration from Mary Washington College. She served as a Peace Corps Volunteer in Uzbekistan, is a black belt in Tae Kwon Do, and has been active in many community efforts, including being a foster parent and serving on the board for the Literacy Council of Northern Virginia.

Alan Lee Myers, MA, PCC
www.linkedin.com/alanleemyers

Alan Lee Myers has worked for several federal government agencies over the last 34 years in various roles, including human resource development, training, organization and leadership development, public health, tribal self-governance, consulting, coaching, coach development, and coaching supervision. Alan, along with many other agency coaching program managers, is a Founding Member of the Federal Coaching Network, established by the Office of Personnel Management. He designed, developed, and presently serves as the founding Director of the Federal Internal Coach Training Program (FICTP), an ICF-accredited program awarded "Best Leadership Development Program" in 2014 by the Human Capital Management Group. In 2019, Alan received the Distinguished Service Award for Leadership Development from the Training Officers Consortium. He is also a two-time recipient of the Health and Human Services (HHS) Secretary's Award for Distinguished Service. His vision is to transform the government into a coaching culture. To support the further development of internal coaches government-wide, Alan is in the planning stages of developing a cadre of coaching supervisors. He served as the Co-lead for Government Coaching Community of Practice for ICF Global.

A. Myers earned three Master of Arts degrees in Counseling Psychology, Instructional Systems Development, and Conflict Management. He did additional post-graduate work in Leadership and Management and in Theology. He holds a Bachelor of Science degree in Religion. Alan holds certifications in Hypnosis/Hypnotherapy, Neuro-linguistic Programming, and Time Line Therapy® Techniques, Leadership Coaching, Design Thinking and Innovation, and Coaching Supervision, and Diversity, Equity, and Inclusion. Alan is a Professional Certified Coach (PCC) through the International Coach Federation (ICF). He is passionate about social dancing (salsa, bachata, Kizomba, Urban Kiz, and many others) and how it develops leadership and followership skills for everyone. Another one of Alan's passions is the use of improvisation. He and his improv classmates performed at the Maryland Ensemble Theater in Frederick, Maryland. He resides in New Market, Maryland.

Foreword

It is an honor and privilege to write a foreword for this book written by three powerful pioneers of coaching across the U.S. Federal Government agencies of the United States. I have been watching their progress over the last ten years, through the many challenging stages of developing not just coaching provision, but an integrated coaching culture that can transform public service leadership development and contribute to the transformation of key government provision.

In the United Kingdom, in the second term of Tony Blair's Prime Ministership (2001–2005), I was asked by the central government "Cabinet Office" to help them look at why, despite the largest-ever increased spend on Public Sector Leadership Development, the three-year reviews of government department were still indicating weakness in the senior leadership of every department. What we discovered was that although the Civil Service were still recruiting some of the brightest people graduating from universities, they were promoted for being good at problem solving, complex analysis, policy writing, and executing new programs within their sub-department. But now many of the challenges were "wicked problems" that could not be resolved within one department but required complex systemic thinking and collaboration across different government agencies, local services, and non-governmental agencies, as well as working with best practice innovation across national boundaries.

Besides high levels of IQ, 21st-century public sector leaders needed high levels of EQ (emotional quotient) and relationship skills, and high levels of We-Q. (collective collaborative intelligence), so teams at all levels could function at more than the sum of their parts. Leadership development practices were still seeing leadership as residing in leaders and sending them off one by one to classroom-based education, looking at case studies about what made yesterday's leadership successful.

What was needed was to move from taking individuals away from their work to do training, and instead, take the development to where the leadership was needed, that is in the complex challenges that needed to be addressed by collective leadership working across traditional boundaries (Hawkins, 2017).

In this book, the authors tell the amazing story of the many stages of development of coaching across the U.S. Federal Government. They show how it started from the passion and purpose-driven determination of a few remarkable pioneers. They then well illustrate the recognizable stages of developing a coaching culture (Hawkins, 2012) through:

1. **Developing an accredited panel of accredited coaches** who understand the context of working in government.
2. **Developing internal coaches, mentor coaches, and coach trainers**, both within departments and across federal government.
3. **Developing Peer Coaching**, so leaders and managers can not only receive support in their own development, learning from their current challenges, but also learn and develop coaching skills, through supporting colleagues in other functions.
4. **Linking coaching to leadership development**, so that learning does not stay generic, but becomes customized and personalized to the individual's own challenges and learning style and does not stay theoretical but the individual receives coaching and support to immediately turn their learning into appropriate changed behavior and action in their own sphere of influence.
5. **Linking coaching to organizational transformation and change programs**. These include programs to widen and improve diversity and inclusion, develop employee engagement and well-being, respond to COVID pandemic, and adjust to hybrid working.
6. **Developing ongoing supervision and continuing development for all coaches** (Hawkins & Smith, 2013) so they can reflect on and continually improve the quality of their practice.
7. **Developing appropriate Governance and reporting structures** which both preserve appropriate confidentiality and show the wider benefits of the coaching spend, in the value created for the organization, employees, beneficiaries of the departments, and the taxpayer.

8. **Incorporating the use of technology into both the delivery and management of coaching** (Isaacson, 2021).

The authors recognize there is still further to go and our experience of working with the public, commercial, and "for-benefit" (NGO) sectors elsewhere, we would recommend that important future developments would be:

1. **The development of Systemic Team Coaching** (Hawkins, 2021), so that coaching is enabling collective collaborative leadership, so that all Government teams function at more than the sum of their parts. Also developing a **Team of Team's culture** where the totality of the team's effectiveness is more than the sum of the teams' performances (Hawkins, 2022: 220–241; McChrystal et al., 2015).

2. **Harvesting the Learning**, which is where the organization preserves individual and team confidentiality while collecting the collective themes concerning the organizational culture that emerge across the many different coaching conversations. It includes structures for creating the right reflective and strategizing conversations, with the senior Government leaders, based on the cultural theme analysis, on how these can inform the further development of their organizational culture to better engage and align employees and create greater organizational effectiveness in delivering the strategy (Hawkins, 2012: 99–103).

Never has there been a time in human history where human beings are facing such globally interconnected and complex challenges, way beyond what can be addressed by strong individual leaders. This is a world that requires greater collective leadership at all levels in organizations and governments and much greater collaboration, across departments, organizations, and countries. Leadership must be rethought and developed at all levels beyond anything that has gone before, and this book so well chronicles how this requires well-thought-out and well-implemented coaching strategies and programs at all levels and in all government departments. We owe a debt to these pioneers not only for what they have achieved this but also for sharing it with future generations and other governments.

Peter Hawkins PhD
Emeritus Professor of Leadership Henley Business School
Chairman of Renewal Associates
Bath
UK

References

Hawkins, P. (2012). *Creating a coaching culture*. Open University Press; McGraw-Hill Education.

Hawkins, P. (2017). *Tomorrow's leadership and the necessary revolution in today's leadership development*. Henley Business School. https://www.renewalassociates.co.uk/wp-content/uploads/2017/06/Research-Report-Tomorrows-Leadership-and-the-Necessary-Revolution-in-Todays-Leadership-Development.pdf

Hawkins, P. (2021). *Leadership team coaching* (4th ed.). Kogan Page Publishers.

Hawkins, P. (2022). *Leadership team coaching in practice; case studies on developing highly effective teams* (3rd ed.). Kogan Page Publishers.

Hawkins, P. and Smith, N. (2013). *Coaching, mentoring and organisational consultancy: supervision and development*. Open University Press; McGraw-Hill Education.

Isaacson, S. (2021). *How to thrive as a coach in a digital world*. Open University Press: McGraw-Hill Education.

McChrystal, S., Collins, T., Silverman, D., & Fussell, C. (2015). *Team of teams: new rules of engagement for a complex world*. Portfolio Penguin.

Preface

The authors of this book were involved in the content and the context of the book on many levels: they were part of the story. They possessed the same passion for coaching as many of those described in this book. They believed in the power of coaching to make a difference to both the clients of the coaches and the coaches themselves. The authors shared a desire to give back to their federal government colleagues and their communities. They also shared a curiosity to examine and think about the story, to see what more could be learned and shared from it.

The idea for the book began in 2015, when Dr. Theodora Fitzsimmons and Marykate Behan Dougherty were working on a guideline for coaching that was to be published by the Office of Personnel Management (OPM). They both took on this task voluntarily to assist in the ongoing efforts of Ms. Cassie Brennand, Ms. Julie Brill, other volunteers, and the Chief Learning Officer Council (CLOC). Although the guidelines remained unpublished, Dr. T. Fitzsimmons and M. Dougherty continued to talk about the importance of providing guidelines to the entire federal government, as coaching became more popular. Meanwhile, Alan Myers was the Director of the Federal Internal Coach Training Program (FITCP) and in the throes of re-launching the program for a second year. Dr. Fitzsimmons was also assisting with that effort and marveling at his ability to get so many government colleagues to come together to support the training program. She thought A. Myers was like the "Pied Piper" as he led and celebrated volunteers who gave varying amounts of discretionary time that was graciously accepted by him. And while things did not always go smoothly, FICTP was successfully launched year after year, adding new internal coaches to the federal cadre that had grown into the thousands.

Dr. T. Fitzsimmons, M. Dougherty, and A. Myers crossed paths frequently as they worked to support various coach training efforts in the federal government. In addition, each of them had a long list of individual accomplishments promoting coaching at their own agencies. Dr. Fitzsimmons knew that to make the book what it needed to be, she needed the partnership of M. Dougherty and A. Myers. At one session of FICTP, Dr. Fitzsimmons invited them to join her for lunch and discuss writing the book. They agreed that it was a worthwhile endeavor to honor the pioneers of coaching in government and highlight their successes. They also realized that they each had lessons to share with others who might consider launching internal coaching in the federal government. They thought that these lessons would likely apply to both public and private sector organizations.

Their approach was to interview over 40 current and former federal employees, most of whom had managed coaching initiatives in the workplace beginning in the 1980s. As they conducted the interviews and discussed what they heard, certain themes emerged. The book was shaped by the insights gleaned from these interviews and from the personal experiences of the authors.

Disclaimer

The views expressed in this book are those of the authors and interviewees personally, and they do not necessarily reflect the views of their agencies or the U.S. Government.

Introduction

Coaching, as a way that one person offers assistance to another, has existed for thousands of years as people helped each other learn new things. Using coaching to assist a person to make a personal change, such as in performance coaching, life coaching, and leadership coaching, is relatively new. In the past two decades, the coaching industry has grown exponentially, permeating society and organizations. Internal coaching programs have taken hold in organizations worldwide. It is no great surprise that coaching also made an appearance in the U.S. Federal Government. The reason for its emergence is no doubt that coaching was recognized as a unique way to foster big changes in individuals in a relatively short amount of time. Those who experienced coaching talked about and demonstrated its positive impact. Even the negative judgment that only those who needed to be "fixed" should be given a coach was eventually overcome. Coaching in the federal government grew and became a positive offering in many agencies.

This book talks about the story of coaching in the federal government and highlights important insights and lessons learned from over 40 federal employees involved in coaching initiatives, who were interviewed and asked about their experiences. The interview protocol was simple, comprised of eight questions.

- How did you learn of coaching and bring it into your agency?
- What were the reactions?
- What do you consider to be your largest accomplishment in terms of coaching?

- Coaching has evolved dramatically in the last several years—what are your observations?
- What worked well for you when introducing your coaching program?
- What would you have done differently?
- What did you learn?
- What can others learn from your journey?

What emerged from the interviews were the lessons about what did and did not work for coaching programs. Coaching program managers can use these recommendations like a checklist to better ensure the success of a new program.

What also emerged was the impact coaching had on the various populations involved with coaching. The clients of coaching were shown to benefit from the coaching they received. The organizations hosting the coaching programs were positively affected, demonstrated in survey responses, return on investment studies, and return on expectation studies. It was also interesting to learn how passionate employees became after they became coaches. These federal employees had different, sometimes very unrelated roles in their regular government jobs. Some learned to be a coach through an external training program, paid for by the government or by themselves. Others learned to be a coach through FICTP. It was interesting how all of these individuals came to the same conclusion: coaching needed to be brought into the organizations where they worked.

A third theme that emerged was how the presence of coaching in the federal government was evidence of change. It started with the voices of the many individuals who learned about coaching either by being coached or by becoming a coach. It was not a mandated program dictated by high-level policy. The emergence of coaching started in small bursts of rain that formed puddles. More instances of coaching caused the puddles to form a body of water. Today, the body of water is like a lake with tributaries.

The book presents the lessons learned from the contributions of the federal coach cadre and the thinking of the authors about how to successfully establish a coaching program. Chapter 1 lays the groundwork by summarizing the story of coaching in the federal government. Chapter 2 promotes the importance of making the business case before launching a program. Chapters 3 to 8 consider the components and considerations for building and sustaining a vibrant coaching program. Chapter 9 presents the authors' predictions for the future of coaching in the federal government. Chapter 10 concludes with a discussion of coaching as an instrument of change.

The authors paid tribute to some of the pioneers of coaching in the *Tribute to Pioneers* appendix. These were the employees who made those first bold steps to initiate coaching in the U.S. Federal Government; their passion for coaching launched coaching into this environment. All but one of the pioneers, G. Lee Salmon, were interviewed; their answers to the interview questions are presented in the *Tribute to Pioneers* appendix. The authors also included a second appendix of tools and templates, which serve as models and examples for those interested in building a coaching program. A final appendix provides additional information on how to provide additional coaching services within your coaching program and is called *Expanding Your Portfolio*.

Acknowledgments

This book represents the culmination of efforts of the many people who believe in and share a passion for coaching. The story starts and continues with the work they do as coaches who care about their fellow human beings. It has been a privilege for the authors to have connected with these professionals.

We would like to express our gratitude to the interviewees for their time and consideration in meeting with us and sharing their experiences, wisdom, and recommendations. These include but are not limited to the following people:

Shanda Adams
Cheri Allen
Reina Bach
Denise Bailey-Jones
Christine Baker
Teri-E Belf
Randy Bergquist
Erica Bovaird
Bill Brantley
Cassandra Brennand
Julie Brill
Heidi Cahill
Patrick Chapman
Cynthia Covington

Adam Edwards
Angela Falcini
Lynne Feingold
Tina Frizzell-Jenkins
Angela Graves
Richard Hansen
Richard Herrick
Jerusalem Howard
Mavis Johnson
Elena Juris
Leticia Little
Wesley Long
Brian McNamara
Cindy Mazur
Greg McHugh
Nichole Meade
Scott Muhs
Nova Niece-Smith
Carrie Register-Haley
Amy Rogers
Sue Stein
Rebecca Weber
Mike West
Larry Westberg
Jean Wright
Sheila Wright

We would also like to thank the federal agencies where we have worked and our supervisors who allowed us to manage our time so that we could accomplish our primary missions while promoting coaching throughout the federal government. We would like to thank Dr. Jeff T.H. Pon, the director of OPM, who signed the memo in 2018 endorsing the value of coaching in the federal government. We would like to thank Lee Salmon, posthumously, who paved the way for collaboration in government around coaching. We would like to thank all the federal coaches who selflessly donate their time to partner with their fellow employees as they create and pursue goals, make transitions, improve performance, create balance in their lives, and much more. We would like to thank our coaching industry friends who partnered with and inspired us on this journey: Reese Madsen, Erin and Mike Hutchins,

Chris Wahl, Magda Mook, Maria Lester, Joel DiGirolamo, Peter Hawkins, David Clutterbuck, Karyn Prentice, Elaine Patterson, Sam MaGill, Lynne DeLay, Damian Godvard, Lily Seto, Marcia Reynolds, Lloyd Raines, Neil Stroul, and Frank Ball.

We would like to thank our families who supported us in this process and for the help of Donna Edwards, who used a combination of project management, editorial expertise, and amazing inquisitive insight to help get us to the finish line.

Acronyms

AC	Association for Coaching
ACC	Associate Certified Coach
ACSTH	Approved Coach Specific Training Hours
ACTO	Association for Coach Training Organizations
ADR	Alternative Dispute Resolution
AI	Artificial Intelligence
APECS	Association for Professional Executive Coaching and Supervision
ATD	Association for Talent Development
BCC	Board Certified Coach
BCR	Benefits Cost Ratio
CCE	Center for Credentialing and Education
CDO	Career Development Officers
CEU	Continuing Education Units
CHCO	Chief Human Capital Officers Council
CKA	Coach Knowledge Assessment
CLOC	Chief Learning Officer Council
CMS	Centers for Medicare and Medicaid Services
COMENSA	Coaches and Mentors of South Africa
COP	Community of Practice
COTS	Commercial-off-the-shelf
CPC	Certified Professional Coach
DAU	Defense Acquisition University

DC	District of Columbia
DCPAS	Defense Civilian Personnel Advisory Service
DEIA	Diversity, Equity, Inclusion, Accessibility
DIA	Defense Intelligence Agency
DoD	Department of Defense
EEO	Equal Employment Opportunity
EMCC	European Mentoring and Coaching Council
EPA	Environmental Protection Agency
FCG	Federal Consulting Group
FCN	Federal Coaching Network
FDA	Food and Drug Administration
FEMA	Federal Emergency Management Agency
FEVS	Federal Employee Viewpoint Survey
FICTP	Federal Internal Coach Training Program
FCN	Federal Coaching Network
GG	Government Grade
GS	General Schedule
GSA	Government Services Agency
HCI	Human Capital Institute
HCMG	Human Capital Management Group
HHS	Health and Human Services
HR	Human Resources
HUD	Housing and Urban Development
ICE	U.S. Immigrations and Customs Enforcement
ICF	International Coaching Federation
IHS	Indian Health Services
IRS	Internal Revenue Service
IT	Information Technology
ITA	International Trade Administration
MCC	Master Certified Coach
NASA	National Aeronautics and Space Administration
NGA	National Geospatial Agency
OPM	Office of Personnel Management
OUSDI	Office of the Under Secretary of Defense for Intelligence
PCC	Professional Certified Coach
PIP	Performance Improvement Plan
ROI	Return on Investment
ROV	Return on Value
SCP	Supervisor Certificate Program

SES	Senior Executive Service
TEI	Treasury Executive Institute
TSA	Transportation Safety Administration
USAF	United States Air Force
USCIS	United States Citizenship and Immigration Services
USPTO	United States Patent and Trademark Office
VA	Veterans Administration
VITA	Volunteer Income Tax Assistance
WABC	Worldwide Association of Business Coaches
WES	Workforce Engagement Survey

Setting a Vision

1

At times in a coaching relationship, the client and coach experience a deep listening that creates a powerful sense of trust... Listening and silence are the twins of being; they create and maintain this ritual space. Silence is so rich with possibilities; it is where we can meet, connect, and dance with life.

(Salmon, 2002, pp. 58–60)[1]

When you think about government agencies, what comes to mind? Cutting-edge advancements? Quick movements? Innovation? Change? More likely, you think about policies and processes that are slow to change and non-innovative. This is the story of a phenomenon that defies what you normally think about government. It is the story of coaching in government: how it started and gained momentum and what can be learned from the successful adoption of coaching and applied to other change initiatives.

Coaching began in the federal government when a few pioneers had the vision, commitment, and dedication to identify a need for coaching and to make their vision a reality. Their need was simple: instead of paying for expensive external coaches, create a trained cadre of internal coaches to provide the same services with less impact to the budget and make coaching available to all employees—regardless of their grade or role.

G. Lee Salmon (G.L. Salmon) was one pioneer whose deep desire to bring coaching to the federal government was inspired by his personal journey and vision. (Read about the contributions of Salmon and the other coaching pioneers in the *Tributes to Pioneers* appendix.) The pioneers brought coaching

DOI: 10.4324/9781003218937-1

to the federal government for two reasons. First, they wanted to increase the use of coaching skills in the workplace, a belief in teaching both managers and employees to listen, question, reframe, and empower others to create their own action and accountability plans. Second, they wanted to create a coaching culture across government—one that questions, listens, dreams, and considers options rather than depends on the *status quo*.

Imagine the federal government with a culture that values and uses coaching skills and where senior leaders, managers, and employees:

- explore expectations, needs, opportunities, and challenges with an open mind
- identify options and consider barriers
- design plans with accountability
- listen actively, ask questions, approach daily work with a growth mindset, and empower each other

Coaching can lay the foundation to make this vision a reality. It can transform government to support its employees, meet the needs of its citizens, and fulfil its many missions.

A defining moment for many pioneers occurred when they personally received coaching. Their initial coaching experience was so powerful, they sought to develop coaching skills for themselves and wanted to share the *magic* with others. "This was *it!*" In coaching sessions, they set aside egos, quieted their minds, and listened to their hearts. They explored areas of discomfort, which allowed for reflection. They opened up to personal and professional growth. They realized that coaching was one thing that could make a *difference*!

Coaching creates opportunities for change by helping individuals learn how to become accountable for their dreams. The pioneers who envisioned coaching in government had a big dream, flexible vision, and willingness to watch it unfold.

What Makes Coaching Feds Different?

The International Coaching Federation (ICF) website defines coaching as "partnering with clients in a thought-provoking and creative process that inspires them to maximize their personal and professional potential." Although coaches can coach anyone, some schools of thought suggest coaches are more effective when they understand their client's context. The ICF website lists the Core Competencies that describe the qualities of coaches:

- is sensitive to clients' identity, environment, experiences, values, and belief (Competency A1.2)
- seeks to understand the client within their context which may include their identity, environment, experience, values, and beliefs (Competency B.4.1)
- considers the client's context, identity, environment, experiences, values, and beliefs to enhance understanding of what the client is communicating (Competency D.6.1)

Coaching models, such as systematic coaching with teams (Hawkins & Turner, 2020), also emphasize the importance of looking at a client's context to be a successful coach.

If understanding the client's worldview and story is important, we believe employees in the federal government need coaches who truly understand both them and their context. The effects of bureaucracy, regulation, and the requirement to be non-political in a highly politicized system create challenges. The restrictions and controls on interactions involving financial planning, human resources, procurement, and technology often make simple tasks quite complex. Add to this, the culture of each agency tends to vary. In this unique environment, coaches who are familiar with the working conditions of their clients will be more effective.

The service philosophy of the federal government draws many people to work there. For others, the appeal is job security. Although these employment drivers are found in other organizations, when combined with the described working conditions, the culture of the federal government creates a context that requires employees to possess a special kind of resilience.

Although there is no typical government coaching client, it is helpful to understand the perspective of non-supervisory employees, team leads, supervisors, managers, and senior executives.

Non-supervisory employees are considered individual contributors responsible for managing their own actions and completing tasks.

Team leads monitor other employees for a percentage of their duty time. They generally perform the same type of work as the employees they lead. They may assign work, provide training, offer feedback, and monitor progress. They are typically the liaison with the supervisor.

Supervisors/Managers have authority to hire, direct, provide performance appraisals, and assure tasks are completed.

Managers of Managers generally have supervisors and/or managers reporting to them. Depending on the agency, they may play a more strategic role in defining culture and developing strategy.

Senior Executive Service (SES) members serve as the executive management of federal agencies. They are responsible for aligning agencies with the administration's focus. They set strategy and oversee implementation at a high level.

Having a contextual understanding of government hierarchy, culture, and leadership experiences enables internal or external coaches to better serve their government clients.

Coaching Pioneers

Organizations in the federal government began using coaches in the 1980s. During this time, talent development professionals had discovered coaching and were incorporating it into their practices. Many pioneers brought coaching to their organizations for the professional development of senior leaders via contracts for outsourced coaches.

Although the private sector adopted coaching earlier than the federal government did, by the early 2000s interest was growing and a few agencies had established coaching programs. Founded in the mid-1990s, the Department of Education (DOE) Coaching Program was the earliest program we documented that used external coaches to support executives and senior leaders. Cheri Allen (C. Allen), an early pioneer who became a key contributor in several cross-governmental coaching programs, was introduced to coaching when she became the coaching program manager at DOE in 2000. In a few years, C. Allen developed coaching at DOE into a respected program with a significant budget. During this time, she presented at the Excellence in Government conference on the benefits of coaching for leadership development. C. Allen also recalled that sometime in 2005, *The Government Training News* published an article on how coaching strategically develops leaders, noting that the coaching program at DOE was "novel" within the federal government.

Along with leadership development, coaching also emerged as a part of programs that supported conflict resolution and career support. In the early 2000s, the Veterans Administration (VA) began training doctors to use coaching skills. This unique program won an Association for Talent Development (ATD) award for training skills and became a model for the Federal Internal Coach Training Program (FICTP). National Aeronautics and Space Administration (NASA) established a coaching program as part of its leadership development activities and the Federal Emergency Management Agency (FEMA) introduced coaching in its conflict resolution office. Some programs survived, others did not. Regardless, coaching was beginning to take root.

Most agencies started coaching programs with contracts for external coaches. In 2006, Gordon Lee Salmon (G.L. Salmon), with the assistance of C. Allen, established the Federal Consulting Group (FCG) Coaching program, a fee-for-service entity that enlisted a cadre of contract coaches to provide coaching to federal agencies that were unable to establish their own programs. G.L. Salmon hosted occasional meetings for coaches and clients, and through networking and educating, he spread his belief that coaching conversations transformed individuals and their organizations and encouraged others to become coaches.

As more federal employees trained to become coaches, they brought coaching to their organizations and coaching responsibilities were typically added to their existing roles, such as leadership trainer or conflict mediator. Many were the only coaches in their organizations and they sought out colleagues in other agencies. In the mid-2000s, a small group of coaches from several agencies informally found each other. Led by Lynne Feingold (L. Feingold), the group included C. Allen, Erica Bovaird (E. Bovaird), Susan Collins, and others. They provided coaching to their organizations, collaborated to support each other's programs, and supported each other's professional growth and learning. When L. Feingold asked them to coach employees from each other's agencies, these coaches became the first cross-agency internal coaching cadre although they were not part of an official program. L. Feingold clearly remembers E. Bovaird saying, "You want me to coach people who aren't in my agency?" and asking L. Feingold for clarification, because providing services across agency boundaries was not the norm.

The cadre informally supported each other and coached for a couple of years. During this time, coaching expanded, as if everyone in government was having the same idea at the same time, planting coaching "seeds" that blossomed over the years.

Coaching Consortium

In 2009, based on the experiences and lessons learned of the smaller cadre and wanting to form a more established group, L. Feingold launched a coaching consortium to share coaching best practices. Her vision for a government-wide coaching culture included eventually sharing coach services across all agencies. She shared an excerpt from the group's Coaching Consortium Charter.[2]

- We are committed to bringing together coaching leaders within federal agencies to discuss strategic challenges and opportunities related to running a coaching program and at the same time, attending to broader goals such as collaboration between agencies, innovation in developing leaders, and identifying efficiencies within government. More specifically, to provide a forum to:

- share best practices, resources, and technologies related to coaching
- increase collaboration among federal agencies through coaching
- discuss pertinent issues, challenges, and opportunities in running an effective coaching program

During a 2009 Treasury Executive Institute (TEI) governance meeting, Jean Wright (J. Wright), an early adopter of coaching at the Office of Thrift Supervision, and an executive who had been inspired by his coaching experience, suggested TEI provide coaching services to their membership. The governance group established a committee to explore the concept. In March 2010, J. Wright and several committee members including L. Feingold presented their findings and the TEI governance board approved the recommendation. J. Wright noted the enthusiasm, passion, and sponsorship of the executives and the vision of the committee were instrumental in initiating the first official cross-agency coach program. While the program was internal to TEI, the coaches were external to the organizations of the coachees. To expand the cadre of coaches and foster a coaching culture, the vision included coach training, continuing education, and a repository of resources for coaches and coachees. The program partnered with their membership to support and supplement bureau programs, not to replace those internal coaching programs.

Committee member L. Feingold leveraged many of the coaches from the initial coaching consortium and the vision from the committee to implement the coaching program at TEI. When she began marketing the coaching program, she did not know what to expect and was overwhelmed with the number of responses. Clearly, the community had keen interest in coaching.

L. Feingold also wanted to pilot a cross-agency peer coaching program for SES members. She realized that although one-on-one coaching was powerful, peers using coaching skills to help peers would create faster cultural change across the federal government. For these efforts, L. Feingold was asked by ATD to write the article, Unleashing the Power of Peer Coaching.[3]

The Office of Personnel Management (OPM) was the next significant player to support coaching in the federal government. In December 2012, OPM released the *Executive Development Best Practices Guide*, which compiled research and findings from interviews with leading organizations on the professional development of executives and highlighted a common disparity between private and public sectors. In private industry, executive coaching was an integral part of leadership development, compared to the federal government, where it was often used as a remedy for poor performance or to close competency gaps. For Julie Brill (J. Brill), Director for Leadership and Executive Development at OPM, this report put coaching on her radar. The report and other research she led highlighted how coaching was one of the most effective leadership development activities. At the same time, several coaches across government, including several from the 2009 Coaching Consortium, were discussing the future of coaching in government and looking for ways to garner support. The Coaching Consortium submitted a paper on the possible future of coaching and shared it with J. Brill. This interest and initial work spurred OPM to increase sponsorship of coaching efforts, strengthened by the leadership of Cassandra Brennand (C. Brennand), Program Manager of Leadership Development at OPM, who with J. Brill worked diligently to gain support of the Chief Learning Officer Council (CLOC).

Internal coaches were emerging all over the federal government. An interesting characteristic of this cadre was that they often sought out each other, shared best practices, and spoke about the uniqueness of the federal government environment and how delivering coaching aligned to their strong shared commitment to public service. There was camaraderie in the coaching community growing in the federal government.

Title: Unlocking a Federal Coaching Culture, C. Brennand (2017)

Brennand 2017 ATD Magazine Article "Unlocking a Federal Coaching Culture"

C. Brennand wrote for *ATD Magazine* in 2017 (https://www.td.org/magazines/the-public-manager/unlocking-a-federal-coaching-culture):

- Over the past three years … the U.S. Office of Personnel Management (OPM), in partnership with the Chief Learning Officers Council, has established and grown the Federal Coaching Network, a community of individuals bound by a mission to foster a culture of coaching across government. The network identified four initial objectives:
- develop a federal internal coach training program
- build a database of coaches in government and share services between agencies
- conduct a return on investment (ROI) study to determine the value of coaching
- create coaching guidance and policy

Federal Coaching Network

Both J. Brill and C. Brennand often presented about coaching at CLOC meetings. After one annual strategic planning session, J. Brill made a proposal to the CLOC to include a goal to put together a strategy to expand coaching in the federal government. The CLOC agreed and included metrics for the goal of how many employees were trained as coaches and how agencies could leverage existing coaching cadres. After all, agencies were spending a lot of money on coach training and OPM wanted to ensure that agencies had access to these assets. In 2012, J. Brill and C. Brennand convened a meeting of coaching program managers from the major departments and agencies.

Called the Upper Room Meeting (due to its location in a top floor conference room at OPM) and attended by representatives from Health and Human Services (HHS), Defense, Commerce, Interior, Labor, General Services Administration, Treasury, Federal Housing Financing Administration, and many others, it resulted in the creation of the Federal Coaching Network (FCN). Based on input from CLOC, OPM had identified three pillars or purposes and the exuberant attendees to the Upper Room Meeting added a fourth:

1. create a database of trained coaches across government
2. collect data on return on investment (ROI) of coaching
3. create a guidance document for agencies standing up coaching programs
4. develop coach training

The CLOC enthusiastically approved the four pillars of the FCN mission and embraced coaching as a developmental tool for the community.

FCN Charter

The FCN Charter established FICTP, directed the development of a government-wide database of coaches, and initiated the development of policy about coaching. C. Brennand described the experience in the Upper Room Meeting, "It was like a groundswell; you could feel the passion for coaching in the room and I knew we were going to create something incredible together."[4]

FCN Charter

Who. A network to support and coordinate Federal coaches across agencies.

What. This network will be guided by a framework designed to build a shared coaching environment across government: 1) determine the value of coaching, 2) build a database of coaches in government and share services between agencies, 3) develop a federal internal coaching training program, and 4) create coaching guidance and policy.

Mission. To foster leadership development and continuous learning at all levels by leveraging resources to advance coaching across agencies.

Vision. Transforming government to navigate the complexity of the 21st century by encouraging innovation and accountability.

Who Benefits? The benefits of a shared coaching program extend far beyond cost savings, to include agencies being able to build their internal coaching capacity and increase employee engagement by creating more effective leaders. Training internal coaches and sharing services between agencies demonstrates a renewed commitment to interagency collaboration and investment in the development of leaders at all levels. As an added benefit, the FCN was also an investment in the development of our coaches, who used those skills in their roles within their respective agencies.

Federal Internal Coach Training Program

Alan Myers (A. Myers) led the "big hairy audacious goal" to adapt the HHS Bootcamp and create an ICF-approved coach training program that was created for federal employees and delivered by federal employees.

A. Myers had long envisioned coach training "for feds, by feds," since his work with Indian Health Services (IHS) from 1993 to 1999. His degree in counseling psychology with an emphasis in Adlerian psychology and his role as an internal organization development consultant and lead leadership development trainer led him to use "coaching" as a fundamental skill. In 2005, he completed the Georgetown University Leadership Coaching Certificate. In 2009, when he landed a job at HHS Office of the Secretary, the idea for FICTP began to form.

In 2013, A. Myers invited C. Brennand to participate in the second offering of HHS Coaching Boot Camp, and she witnessed the successful collaboration between agencies. With CLOC and OPM support, activity increased to create FICTP, and a committee of volunteer coaches from different agencies developed the materials.

In April 2014, the first FICTP was delivered to 80 participants from 23 departments and agencies. Approximately, 32 individuals served as mentor coaches and faculty. The initial program produced 70 coaches and was valued at $12,000 per participant. FICTP became an ICF-approved Professional Certified Coach (PCC) training program and won Best Leadership Development Program by the Human Capital Management Group (HCMG) in 2014.

Emerging Communities of Practice

FICTP began to populate the federal government with certified coaches, who impacted leader development and the productivity and well-being of colleagues across the United States and around the world. Part of their vision was building a community for coaches. Over time, several opportunities emerged organically.

Journal of Federal Internal Coaching. Dr. Denise Bailey-Jones, Health and Human Services (HHS), agreed to be the editor for the *Journal of Federal Internal Coaching*. A few editions were published.

Government Community of Practice. In 2013, Dr. Sue Stein (Dr. S. Stein), then a retired federal coach, approached the ICF DC Metro Chapter to create a special interest group for coaches in the federal government, for both employees and contractors to share best practices and learn from guest speakers. Dr. Richard Hansen was the first lead for the group and Larry Westberg (L. Westberg) became the group leader soon after and continues to lead the community at the writing of this book.

International Community of Practice for Government Coaching. The federal coaches made their international debut in January 2016, when ICF invited A. Myers to co-lead the International Community of Practice for Government Coaching. The group met quarterly for three years and included coaching thought leaders from all over the world.

Coaching Leaders' Forum. In April 2016, TEI collaborated with OPM to establish the Coaching Leaders' Forum. This quarterly meeting brought together coaching program managers from federal agencies to share best practices and resources. Information gathered in this group and shared on OPM's FCN website assists countless program managers, saving them from reinventing the wheel.

Department of Defense Coaching Community Collaboration. The Department of Defense (DoD) established a working group that met monthly to emphasize coaching and coaching culture. Dr. Theodora Fitzsimmons (Dr. T. Fitzsimmons) brought coaching program managers from across the Intelligence Community to several coaching summits to share best practices.

OPM Coaching Memo

Another landmark in the history of coaching in the federal government came when in 2018, the Chief Human Capital Officers Council (CHCO) at

OPM released the memo *Coaching in Federal Government*, highlighting the importance of creating a coaching culture in government. The memo stated, "Coaching is one of the most valuable developmental resources we can offer our workforce and has been linked to positive outcomes such as increased productivity, retention and engagement." The 2018 OPM Memo validated coaching to many agency leaders, assuring them that coaching programs were worth pursuing.

The Opportunity of Coaching

> Never doubt that a small group of thoughtful committed individuals can change the world. In fact, it's the only thing that ever has.
>
> Margaret Meade

Coaching provides an opportunity for government leaders and employees to work under a whole new paradigm—a coach approach to public service. Additionally, it may be an effective way to address diversity challenges in government workspaces. A proven leadership strategy, coaching develops and supports individuals and teams, enabling them to provide exceptional customer service to meet their agencies' missions. Coaching is also a tool that can clarify one's beliefs and values while allowing one to go deeper to acknowledge unseen biases and develop growth mindsets. Thus, coaching byproducts include improved employee engagement, new perspectives, and creative solutions which are needed, and sometimes missing, in today's workplaces.

Title: Interview with Dr. Sue Stein

An Internally Focused External View

Federal coaching started with and has always included external coaches. In fact, great external coaches were instrumental in bringing coaching to the federal government. Some came with just coaching skills, many also had federal work experience.

Many external coaches are interested in supporting the federal government and need to make their own key decisions to plan their approach. These are the same decisions internal coaches make if they decide to start their own business. When working in the federal government, knowing procurement regulations is critical, as well as devising a strategy that works.

Government is big and it is wise to define your coaching niche so you know where to focus. Are you interested in DoD work? Working with the international development community? Do the work needed to define the clients you will best serve.

One of the pioneers of coaching, Dr. S. Stein established her own business after retiring. She found that contracting on her own was an administrative burden, time consuming, and left her less time to focus on coaching. She soon discovered that using her contacts and leveraging relationships was the secret to acquiring clients. She came up with several strategies, noting that as coaching evolves, these will also evolve.

- Join a community of practice supportive of clients in your target audience. There are now several in the federal government coaching communities of practice. When Dr. S. Stein launched her business, they were all just for federal employees, so she worked to launch the ICF Government Community of Practice.
- Contact vendors or subcontractors who hold contracts for leadership development and coaching. If you are a former employee, be mindful of the ethics requirements.
- Create or join a coaching leads project team. Dr. S. Stein established a couple of these. Her favorite model was to create a team of 12, and each month, one of the group members invited a vendor who was involved in government coaching. It's a great way for vendors to meet newly qualified coaches and for coaches to make contacts. The group also shares leads with each other.
- Offer free seminars or webinars. This is best if you target your niche and can be a tremendous way to get referrals.
- Write articles for newsletters and professional publications. Dr. S. Stein recently launched a newsletter, *Friends of Government Coaching,* that provides a great platform.
- Blog. LinkedIn is a great place to share and you can continue to build your contacts through their application.
- Create a group to conduct studies to share with the community. In 2017–2018, Dr. S. Stein established a small group, who researched coaching in the federal government. After surveying and analyzing

the data, they presented the report and posted the results on a website. The group is currently starting a second study.

- Teach for others or establish your own organization. Dr. S. Stein founded the University of Government Training, which offers certificates in Government Coaching and Coaching Executive Core Qualifications.

Establishing a coaching business requires business acumen. Dr. S. Stein stressed that many need to start by finding out where they can get it free or cheap. She learned about the tax laws by volunteering with AARP's Volunteer Tax Aide program (VITA). The IRS has a similar program, VITA (https://www.irs.gov/individuals/irs-vita-grant-program). In addition, she has taken advantage of the Small Business Administration's SCORE program (https://www.score.org), which provides free mentors for business owners.

Dr. S. Stein also stressed that for federal coaches, it is important to build a bridge while in the federal government. Her tips included taking time to keep yourself up to date to obtain certifications and credentials and establish your business (even if it's just a few clients).

Key Takeaways

- Change can happen with committed employees who believe in something bigger than themselves.
- Often it only takes one idea from someone to plant the seed to initiate change.
- Several communities of practice exist to support coaching—find one that aligns with your goals.
- According to OPM, coaching is a valuable developmental resource for the government workforce.

Key Questions

- What is your big dream?
- What are you solving for your organization with coaching?
- What support do you have for the program?
- What can you learn from those who went before you?

References

Brennand, C. (2017, October 10). Unlocking a federal coaching culture. *The Association for Talent Development the Public Manager*. https://www.td.org/magazines/the-public-manager/unlocking-a-federal-coaching-culture

Chief Human Capital Officers Council. (2018, September 10). *Coaching in the federal government*. U.S. Office of Personnel Management. https://chcoc.gov/content/coaching-federal-government

Hawkins, P., & Turner, E. (2020). *Systemic coaching: Delivering value beyond the individual*. Routledge.

International Coaching Federation. (n.d.). Core competencies. Retrieved January 1, 2022, from https://coachingfederation.org/core-competencies

Salmon, G. L. (2002). Coaching and transformational listening. In Belf, T. (Ed.), *Coaching with spirit* (pp. 58–60). Pfeiffer.

U.S. Office of Personnel Management. (2012, December 17). *Executive development best practices guide*. https://www.opm.gov/wiki/uploads/docs/Wiki/OPM/training/OPM%20Executive%20Development%20Best%20Practices%20Guide.pdf

Notes

1 The epigraph by G. Lee Salmon is from the article he wrote for Coaching with Spirit and has been reprinted with permission of the author, Teri-E Belf.

2 L. Feingold provided an unpublished copy of the Coaching Consortium Charter, written and adopted in 2009 by a small group of coaches in the federal government who created a community of practice.

3 The article written by L. Feingold is available on a members only accessible site. See Feingold, L. (2016, October 10). Unleashing the power of peer coaching. Association for Talent Development the Public Manager.

4 The Federal Coaching Network Charter is an excerpt from an unpublished document presented by J. Brill and C. Brennand to the Chief Learning Officer Council in 2012.

Capturing the Business Case

2

> Although senior leaders talked about ROI in terms of money, what really got them excited was the evidence of changes in leader behavior and the stories of value for people.
>
> Larry Westberg

Building the initial business case to secure funding and sharing accomplishments to continue to secure resources are critical for any program, including coaching programs. In our interviews, we found that managers of successful coaching programs were adept at telling their stories and communicating the value or benefit of coaching to the organization. As coaching pioneer Richard Hansen (R. Hansen) shared, coaching programs "often must tell their story over and over and over again."

The evaluation of learning programs has been well defined in the Kirkpatrick Model and applied to coaching in *Measuring the Success of Coaching* (Phillips et al., 2012). This chapter outlines the evaluation process and provides examples of how several organizations successfully implemented return on investment (ROI) studies in their coaching program.

Tell the Program's Story in Dollars and Sense

The key to a successful ROI story is connecting coaching to business value, a daunting task because what is important to each organization is different. For example, what is important to a production facility could be the safety of

DOI: 10.4324/9781003218937-2

its employees. In this case, if coaching can be tied to increased safety, it will absolutely make a business case to invest in or continue to invest in coaching. Examples of items that could be measured:

- increased customer satisfaction
- increased employee satisfaction
- improved productivity
- reduced performance errors
- increased employee engagement
- reducing employee attrition
- increased performance scores in performance appraisals
- increase in promotions
- decrease in employee complaints (EEO or ADR)
- increased employee retention
- improved leadership 360 assessment results

Making a value proposition to those who provide resources for the program about how the program benefits the mission and the goals of the organization is not an easy task. However, some of our interviewees succeeded in doing just that.

Five Levels of Evaluation

Table 2.1 is adapted from the five levels of the Kirkpatrick Model (Phillips et al., 2012). We recommend that managers of coaching programs consider including all five levels of evaluation in their business case strategy.

Focus on Evaluation Levels 4 and 5

Although Evaluation Levels 1, 2, and 3 can all be accomplished with a simple survey, Levels 4 and 5 provide the story about business value. The questions answered for these levels build the case by collecting data to monitor that will help you tell the story.

What data will help? Organizations have data that could already be leveraged as indicators of something. For example, let's say the goal of your coaching program was to increase employee engagement. If your organization conducts an annual survey that asks employees about their level of engagement and you can also identify the individuals who received coaching, you could possibly correlate those two data points.

Table 2.1 Kirkpatrick Model Evaluation Levels and Key Questions

Level of Evaluation	Objective	Key Questions
Level 1 Reaction, satisfaction, and planned action	This level looks at the initial reaction of the coaching clients to the coaching that they received. Reaction data are typically captured after the first two or three sessions or at the end of the coaching engagement.	• Was the coaching relevant to coaching clients' jobs and purpose of their roles? • Was the coaching important to coaching clients' jobs and success? • Did the coaching provide the coaching client with new information? • Do coaching clients intend to use what they learned? • Would coaching clients recommend the program or process to others? • Is there room for improvement with coach selection and match, coaching session duration and frequency, and the setting for the coaching work?
Level 2 Learning	This level captures what the clients have learned from their coaching sessions. These questions can be incorporated in the Level 1 survey mentioned above.	• Did the coaching clients gain the knowledge and insights identified at the start of coaching? • Do coaching clients know how to apply what they learned? • Are coaching clients confident to apply what they learned?

(Continued)

Table 2.1 Continued

Level of Evaluation	Objective	Key Questions
Level 3 Application and implementation	This level evaluates how well clients have applied what they learned (and committed to) during the coaching to their workplace. All evaluation strategies for coaching initiatives should include assessments at this level. These can be accomplished through a survey or interview at a specified time following the conclusion of coaching.	• How effectively are coaching clients applying what they learned? • How frequently are coaching clients applying what they learned? • If coaching clients are applying what they learned, what is supporting them? • If coaching clients are not applying what they learned, why not?
Level 4 Business impact	This level documents the business impact from the coaching initiative. Impact areas include output, cost, quality, and time. This may require multiple avenues of collecting data, including surveys.	• So what if the application is successful—what impact does it make to the business? • To what extent does application of knowledge and insights improve the business measures the coaching program was intended to improve? • How does the coaching program affect output, quality, cost, time, customer satisfaction, employee satisfaction, and other measures? • How do you know it was the coaching that improved these measures?
Level 5 Return on Investment	This level tabulates all monetary benefits: coaching initiatives, factors in full loaded costs of the initiative, and ROI.	• Do the monetary benefits (e.g. impact on budget) of the improvement in business impact measures outweigh the cost of the coaching initiative?

Adapted from Phillips et al., (2012).

It is important to be intentional when collecting and using data. Sometimes, program managers work to evaluate or assess the coaching program, but do not use the data collected. It is also concerning when the items measured do not directly relate to the information needed to tell the story. Identify key metrics that align to and demonstrate the outputs and impacts of the coaching program, considering what is worth measuring and will demonstrate the program's value to the organization. Decide whether the cost of measuring is reasonable. Finally, prepare the business case and be prepared to respond to each stakeholder's questions, addressing their specific needs so that they use the business case to actively support the coaching program and see how coaching supports their needs.

Data Collection Tips

Many program managers ask coaching clients the same questions at the beginning, middle, and end of a coaching engagement, for comparison. Also, having a control group who do not receive coaching services can help with data analysis. Carrie Register-Haley (C. Register-Haley) of United States Citizenship and Immigration Services (USCIS) believes it is best to measure usage of coaching, because "when clients come back or refer you to others, they are voting for the service."

Some program managers attempt to show ROI as a monetary result. For government coaching programs, this strategy can prove challenging because often the monetary impact cannot be isolated. However, if you are focused on winning an award, monetary ROI is often a requirement for submissions.

Many program managers try to capture the benefit of collateral duty and use of discretionary time that energized coaches and propelled them to better performance with their other assigned duties. Remember to capture intangible benefits.

Technology in Program Evaluation

From our interviews, it was evident that government coaching programs lacked availability to specialized technology platforms to assist in data collection. However, we anticipate that such technology will become available. Some private coaching organizations have begun to use technology to capture data about coaching experiences and provide statistics of observable client growth and development. They provide dashboards showing data correlated to stress reduction, resilience, leadership skills, team performance, and retention to organizations. Coaching effects can also be mapped to key Federal Employment Viewpoint Survey (FEVS) indices in the same way.

How Pioneers Told Their Stories

Being able to research, gather data, and perform analysis is important to tell the story, show value, and demonstrate the impact of a program. The challenge is showing what is really happening because impact is hard to measure in isolation. Bill Brantley (B. Brantley) at United States Patent and Trademark Office (USPTO) believes that telling the story is easier when coaching is attached to leadership programs and more challenging for programs that just offer coaching. Here are some examples of how different federal coaching programs showed their value.

Calculating Return on Value and Cost Avoidance at TEI and FITCP

To demonstrate process improvements and return on value (ROV) of the costs to develop employees, TEI program managers gathered data about their coaching services using a simple Level 1 survey distributed to clients at the conclusion of coaching engagements. They tracked responses to the question, "Would you recommend coaching to others?" to gauge the overall success of the coaching program and gathered testimonials from clients. Also, coaches received feedback about their coaching services based on responses collected in this survey.

TEI also tracked coach assignment hours and calculated cost avoidance by using internal coaching services to show the value of their internal coaching program. They computed cost avoidance by multiplying the internal coach assignment hours and the contracted costs for external coaches.

In 2016, C. Brennand at OPM used a similar calculation to determine the ROI of FICTP for a presentation delivered to CLOC:

> (80+30+20+53) coaches trained × $11,500 cost of comparable training = $2,104,500
>
> 183 coaches × 24 coaching hours = 4,392 hours × $200 per hour = $878,400
>
> 955.8 hours coached since February 2015 × $200 per hour = $191,160
>
> $2,104,500 + $878,400 + $191,160 = $3.2 million cost avoidance

This calculation does not account for participant or faculty salaries. If included, this data would further strengthen the cost avoidance business case. In 2020, the approximate cost savings since the beginning of FICTP for all cohorts across the federal government was:

653 coaches trained × $13,500 = $8,815,500

653 coaches × 24 coaching hours (in the program) = 15,672 × 200 per hour = $3,134,400

With an average minimum of 150 hours per coach totaling 97,950 × $200 per hour = $19,590,000

$8,815,500 + $19,590,000 + $3,134,400 = $31,539,900 cost avoidance

Calculating cost avoidance is a valuable measure to stakeholders, which only increases as the coaching program evolves.

Program Performance Dashboard at ITA

Brian McNamara, former CLO at International Trade Administration (ITA), designed a method to demonstrate value when he established their internal coaching program. He selected seven questions from FEVS to use pre- and post-coaching engagements.

- I have opportunities to fully utilize my talents, skills, and abilities every day.
- I have clear personal and professional goals and a plan by which to achieve them.
- I feel valued and respected for my talents and skills that I contribute.
- I am aware of what my core talents and strengths are and how I can best use them.
- Overall, I feel that I have a good work/life balance.
- I have tools, resources, and strategies for addressing challenges, setback, and failures.
- Overall, I feel more engaged.

This approach provided comparative results by showing the percentage of change based on the difference in weighted averages between pre- and post-coaching evaluations for identical questions that coaching clients completed. It was a powerful way to show the impact of coaching using a measure that ITA was always trying to improve.

The ITA Coaching Program also created a coaching program performance dashboard that included financial data to easily track and share information with stakeholders. Program managers calculated the number of coaching hours required to "pay back" the amount ITA had invested in coach training.

Table 2.2 ITA Coaching Dashboard

Overall Initial Target: Coaching Program Hours Provided	700
Total Hours Coached Since Inception	**1,675**
Percentage of Target Reached for Coaching Hours Provided	240%
Average Historic Coaching Hour Cost (~$300)—Average Staff Hourly Pay (~$50)	$250
Total Coach Training/Travel Dollars Invested Since Inception ($)	$165,000
Overall Target: Coaching Dollars Saved—$ Amount	$165,000
Total Coaching Expenditures Saved/Avoided Since Inception ($)	**$418,750**
Percentage of Target Reached for Coaching Dollars Saved	240%
Coaching Program ROI	153%

They calculated the costs to conduct seven to nine months of coaching services that would compensate ITA for the investment in coach training.

Table 2.2 shows an example of how the ITA Coaching Program recouped ITA's investment through cost avoidance of coaching hours. This combined effort showed the value of coaching to both the client and organization. The ITA Coaching Program won an ICF Prism Award in 2020.

Evaluation and ROI Model at DIA

In program briefs to senior leaders, Dr. T. Fitzsimmons, then Program Manager of the Defense Intelligence Agency (DIA) Coaching Program, always included the following data:

- coachee and client feedback surveys (including testimonials)
- coach feedback
- sphere of influence of the coach
- cost comparison of internal versus external coaches
- correlative data from FEVS
- other data reported from DIA stakeholders

To show the value of the DIA Coaching Program, Dr. T. Fitzsimmons employed the Kirkpatrick Model (Phillips et al., 2012).

Level 1: Reaction, Satisfaction, and Planned Action

Program managers gathered Level 1 data with a straightforward client feedback survey that coaches sent to clients at the conclusion of their coaching engagement. The survey used a four-element Likert scale to eliminate neutral responses and provided clients an opportunity to write comments. A sample of the DIA Coaching Survey is available in the Tools Appendix.

Level 2: Learning

The vendor who conducted the DIA Coach Training and Certification program captured Level 2 data using six questions in a survey administered to participants after each of three modules.

1. I received significant value from this training.
2. I see an application of these skills at work.
3. The content was clearly and professionally displayed.
4. The trainers had a thorough understanding of the content.
5. I feel confident in my skills and ability to coach.
6. I would recommend this course to others in the government.

Table 2.3 displays the survey results of the first ten cohorts of the program, conducted by the leadership and performance coaching company ACT Leadership. For each question, participants could provide written responses.

Level 3: Application and Implementation

Dr. T. Fitzsimmons developed surveys for evaluation Levels 3 and 4 using an approach similar to a 360-degree format that was simple and easily replicated. She asked for guidance on this survey from Joel DiGirolamo, Director of Coaching Science at ICF, and Michael Hutchins of ACT Leadership. The questions were influenced by a validated industry survey that ICF was already using.

The Coach Impact Survey I provided a 360-degree review of the impact that becoming a coach had on the employee and the organization. It measured what coaches learned when they returned to the workplace after some time had passed. The survey's questions asked coaches to evaluate how their

Table 2.3 Leadership and Performance Coaching Certification Program Survey Cohort One to Ten Feedback

Average of Eval Questions No. 1–4 & 6

Training Evaluation Criteria

	Module 1	Module 2	Module 3
Cohort 1	4.94	4.97	4.94
Cohort 2	4.85	4.77	4.92
Cohort 3	4.95	4.93	4.98
Cohort 4	4.98	4.89	4.95
Cohort 5	4.85	4.83	4.90
Cohort 6	4.97	4.90	4.94
Cohort 7	4.85	4.83	4.91
Cohort 8	4.88	4.85	4.96
Cohort 9	4.87	4.73	4.94
Cohort 10	4.97		

Average of Eval Question No. 5

I feel confident in my skills and ability to coach.

	Module 1	Module 2	Module 3
Cohort 1	4.18	4.29	4.71
Cohort 2	3.98	4.13	4.36
Cohort 3	4.13	4.08	4.77
Cohort 4	4.25	4.06	4.50
Cohort 5	4.00	4.05	4.32
Cohort 6	3.93	4.08	4.55
Cohort 7	4.14	4.07	4.25
Cohort 8	3.83	4.14	4.57
Cohort 9	3.56	4.09	4.48
Cohort 10	4.11		

Module 1

	1	2	3	4	5	6
	I received significant value from this training	I see an application of these skills at work	The content was clearly and professionally displayed	The trainers had a thorough understanding of the content	I feel confident in my skills and ability to coach	I would recommend this course to others in the government
Cohort 1	4.93	4.89	4.96	5.00	4.18	4.93
Cohort 2	4.79	4.83	4.92	4.98	3.98	4.71
Cohort 3	4.97	4.93	4.97	5.00	4.13	4.90
Cohort 4	5.00	5.00	4.96	5.04	4.25	4.92
Cohort 5	4.78	4.83	4.92	4.97	4.00	4.72
Cohort 6	4.93	5.03	4.90	5.00	3.93	4.97
Cohort 7	4.83	4.82	4.80	4.93	4.10	4.87
Cohort 8	4.93	4.90	4.83	4.97	3.83	4.77
Cohort 9	4.85	4.85	4.83	4.96	3.56	4.85
Cohort 10	5.00	4.93	5.00	5.00	4.11	4.93
Average	4.92	4.91	4.95	5.01	4.14	4.86

Module 2

	1	2	3	4	5	6
	I received significant value from this training	I see an application of these skills at work	The content was clearly and professionally displayed	The trainers had a thorough understanding of the content	I feel confident in my skills and ability to coach	I would recommend this course to others in the government
Cohort 1	4.97	4.90	5.03	5.00	4.29	4.93
Cohort 2	4.74	4.70	4.83	4.87	4.13	4.74
Cohort 3	4.93	4.80	5.00	5.00	4.08	4.93
Cohort 4	4.83	4.96	4.92	4.96	4.06	4.79
Cohort 5	4.81	4.81	4.90	4.94	4.05	4.73
Cohort 6	4.96	4.88	4.83	4.96	4.08	4.88
Cohort 7	4.80	4.83	4.77	4.90	4.07	4.86
Cohort 8	4.82	4.82	4.82	4.96	4.14	4.82
Cohort 9	4.63	4.67	4.67	4.89	4.09	4.81
Cohort 10						
Average	4.87	4.84	4.94	4.96	4.14	4.85

Module 3

	1 I received significant value from this training	2 I see an application of these skills at work	3 The content was clearly and professionally displayed	4 The trainers had a thorough understanding of the content	5 I feel confident in my skills and ability to coach	6 I would recommend this course to others in the government
Cohort 1	4.97	4.86	5.00	5.00	4.71	4.86
Cohort 2	4.86	4.90	4.90	4.95	4.36	5.00
Cohort 3	4.92	4.96	5.00	5.00	4.77	5.00
Cohort 4	4.96	4.92	4.96	4.96	4.50	4.92
Cohort 5	4.88	4.92	4.92	5.00	4.32	4.80
Cohort 6	5.00	4.93	4.90	5.00	4.55	4.86
Cohort 7	4.90	4.83	4.93	4.97	4.25	4.90
Cohort 8	4.96	4.93	4.96	5.00	4.57	4.96
Cohort 9	4.92	4.96	4.96	4.96	4.48	4.92
Cohort 10						
Average	4.93	4.91	4.97	4.98	4.58	4.95

behavior changed once they returned to their regular jobs, how they were different as a leader, supervisor, peer, or subordinate, and how they were different in meetings. A sample of the DIA Coach Impact Survey I is available in the Tools Appendix.

Level 4: Business Impact

After completing Coach Impact Survey I, coaches forwarded Coach Impact Survey II to others in their sphere of influence. The data collected from this second survey measured the impact of coaching on DIA. Every recipient of Coach Impact Survey II evaluated the coach-leader and described how they believed the coach-leader's behavior was affected by the fact that they had become a coach. A sample of the DIA Coach Impact Survey II is available in the Tools Appendix.

Level 5: Return on Investment

The Level 5 ROI that Dr. T. Fitzsimmons presented was notional but impactful. Similar to many coaching programs, DIA hired external coaches for senior leaders enrolled in leadership development courses. If the same 100 senior leader participants were coached by internal coaches, the ROI for DIA was very high. Prior to 2014, the training department hired *external* executive coaches to support the leadership development program: for GG-15s attending Gemstone and for senior leaders attending Great Leaders Great Culture. At an average cost of $430 per hour, DIA spent $347,000 annually to provide coaching to these GG-15s and seniors. Table 2.4 presents the cost comparison for the same number of hours of coaching costs with *internal* coaches.

Missed Opportunity

Dr. T. Fitzsimmons wanted to correlate data from the annual Workforce Engagement Survey (WES) with an increase in internal coaches. From 2016 to 2021, WES data for employee engagement scores and satisfaction with

Table 2.4 The Cost of Coaching at DIA[1]

Coaching Objective	When done by EXTERNAL COACHES	When done by DIA INTERNAL COACHES
Provide 100 GG-15 and SES learners coaching (an average of eight hours each)	$347,000	$20,000

leadership increased as attrition rates steadily decreased. Dr. T. Fitzsimmons wanted to correlate these results to the increase in internal coaches to the program by asking employees "Did you have a coach?" Adding this question to WES would have enabled her to correlate the coaching program's increased usage to positive responses from employees. However, the question was not added to the survey.

ROI Story at USPTO

B. Brantley created a more sophisticated approach to justify a coaching program and demonstrate ROI for a related leadership program when he was at United States Patent and Trademark Office (USPTO). His model shown in Figure 2.1 shows the cyclical approach he believes is necessary to start any program. Using this method, he developed a full business case which defined the environment, the strategic fit and need, along with the scope and necessary capacity of the proposed program.

B. Brantley also identified what success would look like before the Enterprise Training Program's career coaching program formally launched. The identified goals were to demonstrate an 85 percent approval rating by USPTO employees using the services and a significant, sustained increase in five key items on FEVS concerning relations between employees and their supervisors. After receiving funding following the pilot, the coaching

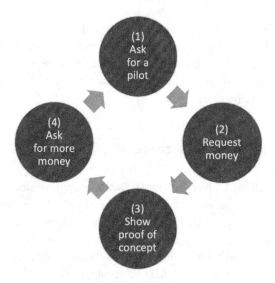

Figure 2.1 Model for Piloting Programs

program managers targeted a 2 percent increase annually. They easily met all goals during the pilot and the program continues to grow.

B. Brantley also proved that the Supervisor Certificate Program (SCP), which taught coaching skills to new supervisors and was supported by the coaching program, was a good investment for USPTO by calculating ROI by using disengagement costs.[2] He also used methodologies outlined in *Measuring the Success of Coaching* (Phillips et al., 2012); although he acknowledged it was difficult to isolate the effects of the program, it provides a compelling case.

> $3,400 for every $10,000 of salary = disengagement cost
> Average salary at USPTO = $123,123
> Average cost of disengagement per USPTO employee = $41,861.82
> The total annual cost to USPTO = $544,203,660
> 70% disengagement = $544,203,660, reduce to 69% = $536,429,322
> Total savings to USPTO = $7,774,338
> SCP contribution (54%) = $4,198,143
> Cost of SCP = $382,568.40

where:

- ROI = (Current value of investment − cost of investment)/cost of investment
- ROI = ($4,198,143 − $382,568.40)/$382,568.40 = 997%
- Benefits cost ratio (BCR) = $4,198,143/$382,568.40 = 10.97

In his interview, B. Brantley shared surveys and testimonials also captured information about the program's intangible benefits, including increased teamwork, commitment, job satisfaction and reductions in conflicts, stress, customer service, and complaints. This data was tracked using FEVS and formal complaint processes.

ROI Story at Defense Acquisition University

Defense Acquisition University (DAU) is the corporate university for the DoD acquisition workforce and a 2012 DC Metro ICF Prism Award winner. Established in 2008, the DAU Coaching Program captured their ROI story in several ways. R. Hansen shared that they often used the research and reports of other coaching and training development thought leaders on the benefits and values of coaching. In addition, DAU employee Dr. Al Mosley researched and used the ROI story of the DAU Coaching Program in his doctoral dissertation, published in *The ROI of Coaching* (Mosley, 2011).

Furthermore, by showing that DAU was investing one-half of 1 percent in the coaching program, R. Hansen believed this justified the program relative to other budgeted items. Finally, they collected and shared client endorsements. One letter shared how a client received coaching around a programmatic knothole and ended up saving $250 million dollars for a multibillion-dollar program. Although anecdotal, it was a powerful story. The DAU Coaching Program story told in their 2012 Prism Award nomination and serves as a model.

Title: DAU Coaching Program 2012 Prism Award Story

DAU Coaching Program 2012 Prism Award Story

The demand for coaching as a preferred talent management modality has tripled. We are now seeing an annual increase in the number of key leaders who express interest in coaching during our executive management courses from 10 percent to 20 to 35 percent. Coaching for these leaders who have been selected to lead major enterprise organizations and major programs is becoming a modality over more traditional learning approaches, including the go-it-alone, trial-and-error approach. Similarly, our portfolio of talent management and leader development courses (e.g., Leader as Coach) remains at maximum capacity for our mid-level managers/supervisors.

Our coaching efforts have been tremendously effective in providing ROE/ROI to our enterprise and workforce. To date, we have coached over 220 key leaders. Many of these competitively selected leaders have assumed duties as portfolio managers, program managers, or key functional leaders of more than 150 major equipment programs and automated information systems. Aware that the demand for our one-on-one or team coaching might outpace the supply of our internal coaches, we created a portfolio of four leadership development courses including a Leader as Coach course for mid-level managers/supervisors. This portfolio has introduced leadership and coaching skills to over 2,700 mid-level managers/supervisors (GS-13 to GS-15) in 128 offerings.

In terms of ROE/ROI, one of our coaches researched and authored a doctoral dissertation and book, *Coaching ROI: Delivering Strategic Value*

Employing Executive Coaching... (2011), documenting qualitative and quantitative workforce development and performance improvements. Client-cited ROE includes enhanced organizational change; improved networking; improved program advocacy (selling the program); becoming a strategic leader/thinker; increased leadership confidence; leader as coach ability; improved employees and career management; more effective stakeholder management; and time management. A Level Five evaluation from our clients reflect:

Level One—Reaction. A positive 92.5 percent value of coaching received, including setting objectives and expectations, rapport, frequency/length of coaching, and 360 feedback

Level Two—Learning. A positive 90 percent value, including working with stakeholders, teambuilding, new perspectives, and leadership effectiveness

Level 3—Application. Top four: improved strategic communication, better change implementation, enhanced stakeholder relationships, and enriched leadership/people interactions

Level 4—Business Impact. Top four: increased self/group productivity, increased customer satisfaction, increased resources, and reduced cycle time

Level 5—Return on Investment. 754 percent. This value is consistent with other independent coaching ROI studies.

Measuring Diversity, Equity, and Inclusion

The ROI/ROE case studies demonstrate how coaching can be a strategy toward meeting an organizational goal. What if it were used to address a common societal problem in the federal government where behavior really matters? We believe that if coaching skills and training are integrated throughout an organization's culture, they will create new awareness of the importance of diversity, equity, and inclusion (DEI) in the organization that will affect the decision making in the organization.

The *2021 State of Diversity Hiring Report*, published by the Human Capital Institute (HCI), lists five key findings.

- Barely Scratching the Surface. Many organizations are missing out on the most basic opportunities to share their commitment to building a diverse and inclusive workforce with potential applicants.

- Working Without a Plan. Many employers' recruitment plans are neither strategic nor specific enough to move the needle.
- Budgets Haven't Budged. Employers aren't adequately funding their DEI initiatives in line with their publicly stated goals. Meaningful progress requires aligning investment with intent.
- Neglecting Opportunities for Internal Talent. Fair and competitive internal hiring plays a critical role in DEI success, yet many organizations are failing to engage the diverse employees they already have.
- Bias Keeps Creeping In. Fair hiring processes add perspective, consistency, and structure to the hiring process, ensuring that all hiring touch points minimize bias. However, many employers have yet to adopt known best practices for minimizing bias in recruitment and promotion.

(Smart Recruiters, 2021)

An organization can look at these findings and consider where having coaching can make a difference. If DEI becomes truly important to the organization, leaders may identify a goal and create a hypothesis around it. For example, if the organization's goal is to increase DEI in recruitment and promotion, the hypothesis could be "If hiring managers and recruiters possess coaching skills, there will be more diverse new hires and more diversity in promotions." The assumption is that with coaching skills, the hiring managers consistently behave in the following manner, both in interviews and with employees:

- listen to the person in front of them
- ask questions in a curious way
- cultivate empathy, compassion, and appreciation for their fellow human beings

Possible measures for data collection could include the following statements:

- monitoring the demographics of new hires and those who are promoted
- interviewing or surveying new hires to ask them what attracted them to the organization
- interviewing or surveying those who participated in hiring panels to see if they have official training in coaching or coaching skills

If you believe, as we do, that coaching has the potential to influence societal issues like DEI, we invite you to consider the above approach for your own organization. The ITA Coaching Program borrowed five questions from FEVS to see if those who received coaching had a positive experience. One goal was to see significant, sustained increase in the five FEVS items concerning relations between employees and their supervisors. Of all of the programs that we reviewed this one was the closest to addressing how coaching can change how employees feel.

Key Takeaways

- Continually share your story in many ways, on various platforms.
- Be prepared to tell your story repeatedly. Since government organizations are not concerned about profits, traditional ROI models may not always fit.
- Both quantitative and qualitative data are critical. The data needs to be backed up by a compelling story of value to both the individual and the organization.
- Develop a clear goal for measuring ROI, i.e., cost, value, funds saved, increased engagement, etc.
- There is no one right formula for calculating return on investment/ value, but it needs to make sense to the organization's leaders both quantitatively and qualitatively.
- Consider key challenges that your organization has where coaching might make a difference.

Key Questions

- What are the goals for the program? How can they be measured?
- What surveys does your organization do every year? What data can you identify that might be affected by the presence of coaching?
- What are the business needs of the organization?
- How can you relate your story to what stakeholders want?
- What resources do you have?
- What staffing (and skill) is needed to support this effort?

References

Mosley, A. (2011). *Coaching ROI: Delivering strategic value employing executive coaching in defense acquisition.* Xlibris Corporation.

Phillips, P., Phillips, J., & Edwards, L. (2012). *Measuring the success of coaching: a step-by-step guide for measuring impact and calculating ROI.* ASTD Press.

Smart Recruiters. (2021, October 12). *From good intentions to lasting impact state of diversity hiring report 2021.* Human Capital Institute. https://www.hci.org/research/2021-state-diversity-hiring-report

Notes

1   In Table 2.4, Costs of Coaching at DIA, the costs presented include the cost of training eight internal coaches.
2   There is an assumed cost to disengaged employees because they are less productive than their fully engaged counterparts.

Overcoming Challenges

3

You have to believe in it and have experienced it yourself in order to have the perseverance, stamina, and the determination to push through the barriers to keep forging ahead.

Cheri Allen

The pioneers discussed in Chapter 1 were committed to coaching and convinced, based on personal experience and insight, that adding coaching to government agencies would change culture and better enable mission. These initiatives were led by powerful personalities, who had funding and a generally accepting climate. However, coaching was new, little understood by agency leadership, and the pioneers faced many challenges. Some initiatives succumbed to the challenges; others persevered. We started our examination of coaching programs formed in the 1990s and early 2000s to understand which were apt to survive or not and discovered that coaching initiatives popped up in a variety of federal agencies based on different circumstances. Underpinning all of these was the fundamental and passionate belief of the program managers and some senior champions that coaching was a catalyst for change worth pursuing.

In our interviews, we searched for patterns that would indicate the reasons for the success or failure of a coaching program and found no clear answers. In the earlier programs, coaching usually emerged as part of another existing program. Funding and budgets for these early efforts were non-existent at first. One pattern was clearly indicated that funded coaching programs were always first on the budget chopping block. Attitudes and beliefs around coaching also

DOI: 10.4324/9781003218937-3

played a part. The motivation for supporting or canceling programs aligned more with the priorities and agendas of the individuals in charge. When a senior executive champion truly believed in the power of coaching, it took hold and received funding and support. Unfortunately, when that champion departed the agency, the coaching program diminished and sometimes shut down. When coaching programs were advocated by mid-level managers who passionately believed in the value of coaching for the development of people and culture in organizations, their belief and perseverance ensured the program's success, but only for the period in which they had the ear of senior leadership. In many cases, time was not a friend of early federal coaching programs. Within months or years of being created, once leadership and agency priorities changed, inevitably the coaching program was no longer supported.

While waning sponsorship and changing priorities were key challenges, we identified other barriers that stood in the way of successful programs. In this chapter, we explore some of the challenges of pioneers, including some that programs continue to face today. Addressing these challenges early on and being mindful of their continued presence can help a program endure.

Misalignment to Mission

The federal coaching programs emerging in the 1990s and early 2000s grew out of programs for conflict management, career development, or leadership development. The pioneers were trying to suggest ways to bring general coaching into an existing effort. These earlier attempts aligned with conflict management and career development eventually met with resistance.

Several interviewees told us about attempts to offer regular coaching in addition to conflict coaching and career management at their agencies. The conflict coaching program managers recognized that providing positive, goal-oriented coaching services to employees *before* they were in conflict would benefit the organization. Another pioneer reasoned that career advisors with coaching skills could first help employees explore essential information about themselves—who they are, their values, their motivations, and their skills. Once employees had answered these baseline questions about themselves, career advisors could better advise them on specific steps to take to achieve their goals. Unfortunately, these attempts did not survive scrutiny. Frequently, coaching services were viewed as "scope creep" and not supportive of the originally funded mission, policies, or expectations of leadership. Essentially, these passionate pioneers of coaching could no longer offer regular coaching because it was deemed an *unauthorized activity*.

In both the conflict and career management program examples, coaching was determined to be a service that hindered the primary function. Although the early pioneers in these offices believed their missions would benefit by including general coaching, they needed to make a very strong business case to expand the original services of their offices. Change in government is like turning an enormous cruise liner, it is not easily made. Even after agency leadership makes a decision, putting the new decision into place can take years. Without a strong case to justify funding for general coaching, the programs we discovered were asked to stop offering coaching and to resume their original functions.

Looking back on the experiences of our early pioneers who wanted to integrate coaching into conflict and career management programs, the authors agreed with their intention and what they tried to accomplish. As coaching grows in popularity, we have some alliances with career development and conflict management being better supported by federal agencies.

Negative Attitudes and Beliefs about Coaching

Early coaching programs struggled because their reputations suffered from misconceptions about what coaching was and misunderstandings that it was primarily for remediating poor performance. C. Brennand talked about research she conducted for OPM in 2016 and 2017, to discover best practices in leadership development across government. While she found coaching to be a best practice, she noted it was implemented inconsistently across agencies, due to some of these attitudes. For example, coaching was viewed as something offered to employees with poor performance and as last-ditch efforts by management before issuing a performance improvement plan (PIP) or some other disciplinary action. As pioneer Randy Bergquist (R. Bergquist) shared:

> Many times, in the federal government, the perception of coaching was that it was used for performance improvement and not as development purposes. This tended to create a negative perception of coaching. While in private industry, coaching was looked at as an incentive/ investment for the stars or high achievers. In other words, when one became a manager and moved up the chain to be an executive, the private industry concept was to give that person a coach, thus investing in that person's future with the organization.

Others in the federal government believed all coaching was life coaching and inappropriate for the workplace unless topics could be controlled and focused on the work at hand. In the conflict management example, leadership viewed conflict coaching to have a work-based purpose but objected to general coaching because they believed it was not serious or workplace appropriate. Also, the word "coach" was generally misunderstood. "A sports coach? Or a mentor?" To add to the confusion, some in the federal government held the opinion that they were coaches and offered coaching to others with no professional accreditation or training.

Early federal coaching programs faced these misconceptions. When a program succeeded, the program manager and senior sponsor(s) educated the organization about what coaching was and was not, along with its benefits. As coaching was recognized in both private and public sectors as a skill useful far beyond remedial performance correction, the acceptance of coaching programs in the federal government increased, ensuring other emerging coach training programs had staying power. Ongoing efforts to educate about coaching services were critical to the success of coaching.

No Home for Coaching

Another barrier to success was the fact that coaching did not have a natural fit in an organization. In the federal government, coaching was frequently classified as training, usually not mission critical, and therefore vulnerable to funding cuts. However, all agencies must fund certain overhead functions, such as human resources (HR) and essential training, to enable their missions. Coaching was not part of any routine HR function; it was a new internal service with no existing policies or home within an organization. While generally found in HR, it was not integrated into the HR mission. Although it will take time and be an uphill battle, we believe coaching will become a permanent program in the federal government with a designated home.

Lack of Policy

In government, the most important thing program managers can do for sustainability is to create a policy for the programs that they want to prioritize for the workforce. Federal policies are very formal documents. They are typically based in U.S. federal law and therefore considered very important and central to whatever the policy addresses.

As much as policies are powerful when they exist, they are also very difficult to put into place. Dr. T. Fitzsimmons recalled her struggles to establish an organizational-level coaching policy at DIA. While she thought an organization-wide policy made perfect sense, convincing her management chain and those who managed policies for DIA was extremely challenging. After years of effort, DIA still did not have an organization-wide coaching policy. Consequently, if an employee at DIA wanted a coach or wanted to become a coach, their supervisor could say that DIA had no requirement for either coaching services or for coaches.

The DIA Coaching Program is codified in an administrative instruction owned and managed by the training department. While not an organization-wide policy, it has been helpful to the program and defined the roles and responsibilities of the program manager, coaches, clients, and the supervisors of both. The problem is its placement. Housed in the training department, it is not easily accessible to DIA workforce. This weakens the policy. A template for a policy document is included in Appendix 2.

For over 20 years, coaching existed in the federal government with no formal policy. Finally, the 2018 OPM Coaching Memo gave coaching much needed credibility, ensuring that coaching programs in the federal government were here to stay. The story of how it came to be is in Chapter 4. This memo was not policy, but it gave agencies permission to perform coaching and was a first step toward creating a formal policy.

Lack of Infrastructure

In interviews, lack of infrastructure was often identified as a weakness among coaching programs. By infrastructure, we mean the software system to house program data, list coach information, conduct client–coach matching, log coaching hours, and provide information to prospects, clients, and coaches. We acknowledge that in the larger federal system, buying or building software platforms is challenging. In addition to the need to secure funding, agencies must address many regulations regarding the purchase and implementation of software and commercial-off-the-shelf (COTS) products. Also, meeting security requirements can be expensive, and some agencies prohibit external products inside their firewall.

Although acquiring a software system was an obstacle few early coaching programs overcame easily, the programs that had them were more successful and offered clients a computer-based mechanism to find coaches easily without the intervention of a person to vet and match them to a coach. Although a manual approach was possible for small programs, it could quickly overwhelm and become inefficient. At EPA, Becky Weber (B. Weber) proved this by working with the Information Technology (IT) department to develop a SharePoint site that allowed the manager to process requests and coach assignments electronically and collect data on engagements. Automating this administrative task improved the coaching program at EPA by decreasing the time required to manage this necessary administrative task.

Coaching program managers, regardless of where they sat in their organization, often did not know where to start to put a software system in place. In addition, pioneers described "building the plane while flying." This approach often damaged the credibility of the coaching program, led to staff burnout, and resulted in rework or lost data.

We recommend developing a strategy for acquiring the necessary systems and establishing partnerships with departments that will support the program's infrastructure strategy, including:

- Internal stakeholders to include in planning, such as the IT department.
- Internal stakeholders who benefit from the coaching program, such as leadership training programs, or executive services.   .
- External organizations interested in collaborating.

As part of the strategy, prepare to answer questions about the coaching program's needs and wants, map your processes, and establish requirements. What are the initial needs of the program and how will they grow as the coaching program evolves? Table 3.1 presents some of the functions included and the workflow that helped to automate coaching processes at DIA, making it less tedious to manage.

Table 3.1 Map of Coaching Processes to Automate at DIA

Process	Description	Workflow
Application to become a coach	DIA employees who are interested in becoming a coach and attending the training complete this application.	When the employee submits the application, it goes to the employee's supervisor. When the supervisor approves it, it comes back to the Coach Program Manager. When the participant completes the program, the record is moved to the list of coaches.
Request a coach	Employees seeking a coach review profiles and selects a coach.	The employee requests a particular coach directly. The coach receives the application and accepts or declines the coaching engagement. The system sends emails to the coach and employee, keeping them informed of the process.

Table 3.1 Continued

Process	Description	Workflow
Coaching log	As coaches do coaching, they update their hours in their coaching log.	The log is configured to be the same as the ICF Coaching Log, enabling coaches to bulk import or export the log as necessary.
Announcements/ events	Simple announcement and calendar of events.	Keeps coaches informed about important information and learning opportunities.
Resources	A repository of resources for coaches.	Coaches are able to share their own resources.

It is also essential to think long-term when considering solutions. What are the pros and cons of the possible solutions? What could go wrong? The coaching program managers at one program made the mistake of linking their coach tracking software to their external website. At the time, this seemed the best decision, to create one system supported by one vendor. Unfortunately, the vendors' primary business was website development and the needs of the coaching system were always an add-on requirement. Also, due to the marketplace from 2016 to 2020, the organization implemented three new websites, which meant the coaching program was forced to implement three new tracking systems to collect hours and manage assignments. This created rework for the program manager and adjustments for the coaches. In 2021, leadership decided to separate the two systems.

Infrastructure Lessons Learned at DIA

At DIA, even if funding had been available, security restrictions made it nearly impossible to use a COTS product; therefore, the coaching program automated processes using SharePoint.

As of this writing, the DIA Coaching Program uses SharePoint to manage all aspects of the program. Particularly handy are the workflows built to enable automation of otherwise time-consuming processes. SharePoint can have various levels of permissions and at DIA, the public sees a very short menu of items to find a coach, find how to become a coach, and find more about the coaching program. The coaches have additional permissions to see resources and log their hours. Finally, the program managers have access to back-end data.

Figure 3.1 shows the home page of the DIA Coaching Program created with SharePoint. The initial challenge was finding someone to design, build, and maintain it, which at first involved begging for internal resources. A contractor was initially available but was not permanent, and support was up and down. At the end of the day, Dr. T. Fitzsimmons stated, "We could not have built and maintained the coaching program without SharePoint."

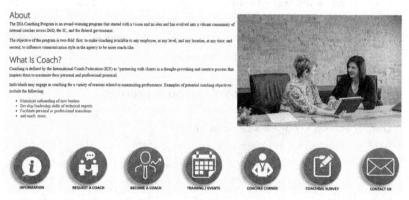

Figure 3.1 DIA Coaching Homepage SharePoint Site

Building or procuring a software system usually involves the IT department, which will have a formal planning and development cycle. The key message is to realize that planning for a software system is crucial for the success of the program, but it can be a difficult and long process to secure software in the government. Therefore, submit your request to the IT department as soon as possible.

No Business Case and No Funding

In the early days, funding was often a barrier. If an organization with a budget for external coaches suddenly had funds eliminated, the program ended, and this made sense because external coaches were—and are—expensive. In these situations, funding for coaching continued for only the most senior agency leaders, usually tied to 360-degree assessments. Offering general coaching to lower-grade employees was cost prohibitive.

Often, we found that no business case was made when programs were established. Many of the coaching activities of the last decade (e.g., FICTP, coaching across government as a part-time duty) were due to the sheer passion, motivation, and vision of pioneers rather than because coaching was a funded activity.

The passion takes the place of funding in this case. According to A. Myers, "It's not a zero-sum game." He offers a possible equation:

$$\$\$ + \text{Vendor} = \text{Federal Employee Motivation, Passion, \& Vision}$$

The value that employees brought to coaching in the federal government was unexpected and welcomed, helping many programs initially overcome lack of funding, although most found passion-driven programs unsustainable.

Title: One Coaching Program's Lessons Learned

One Coaching Program's Lessons Learned

A. Myers learned many lessons for sustaining a vibrant coaching program at the Centers for Medicare and Medicaid Services (CMS), a department of HHS Operating Division. He had been coaching on and off for many years; at CMS, he had the opportunity to develop a formal program.

Coaching at CMS started when A. Myers, who was completing his Georgetown Leadership Coaching Certificate Program, needed to practice coaching with four clients. He was deeply involved in leadership training at CMS, having developed courses and teaching Leadership in Context. A common challenge in leadership development is the ability of participants to generate lasting behavioral change. Participants would opine that while the training was great, implementing newly learned ideas was hard. They blamed the organizational culture for their inability to transfer newly acquired behaviors into the workplace. After hearing these and other complaints from both participants and managers, A. Myers decided the missing piece was lack of personal attention to participants, who needed more one-on-one support as they began trying to behave differently and become more effective leaders. A. Myers used this premise to "sell" coaching to CMS leadership program participants. Once they completed training, he offered to coach them—give personal attention and guidance when they returned to their jobs and implemented new leadership skills in the "heat of battle."

At this stage, coaching was not an official CMS program and only his immediate boss knew it was included in the leadership development curriculum. Coaching remained undercover and clandestine.

When participants heard about the coaching opportunity, they were pretty excited and also a little wary because they did not know what to expect. Other participants heard about the coaching service and requested it. By the time A. Myers had completed his program at Georgetown University, he accumulated over 20 coaching clients. He also was beginning to understand what CMS employees were dealing with on a daily basis.

The personal stories of transformation resulting from coaching in the leadership development program began to get the attention of CMS executives. Once the executive in charge of management operations learned about it, the CMS Coaching Program was officially launched.

The clandestine approach that "it is easier to ask for forgiveness than permission" can be good to try something new, but not for managing and measuring its organizational impact. A. Myers briefed senior leaders on coaching, the results it was delivering to CMS supervisors, and proposed a pilot program with an evaluation. This pilot included the results demonstrated with the 20 coaching clients coached by A. Myers and with the three senior executives coached by a contract coach. The criteria used to evaluate the program was clients' perception of their personal growth and development, the support they received from their coach, and whether they met their personal goals as a result of coaching. The evaluation results of the pilot were positive in all three areas.

The CMS Coaching Program successfully delivered both internal coaching and contract executive coaching services from 2005 to 2009. In a given year, CMS allocated at least $100,000 to contract coaching for executives. A. Myers continued to manage a clientele of approximately 20, which included senior executives, senior managers, first-line managers, and intact teams. In 2009, due to reorganization, shifting priorities of leadership, and A. Myers leaving CMS for another position, the coaching program disbanded. In 2014, coaching returned to CMS when employees were trained at FICTP.

Lessons Learned
Some key reflections from this experience.

- Organizational priorities can shift at a moment's notice, often for unknown and mysterious reasons.
- Coaching programs need to be flexible, agile, and resilient.

- Senior leadership support is not always needed for a program to get started and survive the pilot stage, but it is certainly needed for it to be viable and sustainable in the long-term.
- Coaching requires a senior leader to be accountable for the results of the program and to ensure it remains aligned with the organization's mission.
- The more a program is aligned to mission and clients who say the program is transformational, the harder it is to cancel by new leaders not invested in it. (Though this is not an absolute truth, because a program can still be cancelled even when it is successful. Having more than one person support a program is best.)
- More trained and committed coaches can keep a program alive when the major player leaves or is moved to another position.
- The program needs to be part of the operation and the organization needs to demand it as a service supporting the mission.
- The ROI/ROE is really important, along with communicating the stories of transformation by influential clients.

Key Takeaways

- It is difficult for an enthusiastic coach to independently decide to insert coaching as an additional offering to a program that is funded for a different purpose. (See Chapter 2 for how to make a business case.)
- Beware of negative attitudes and beliefs about coaching.
- Coaching is not yet an official offering in the federal government and does not have a natural home in the organization.
- Without a technology dedicated to the management of the coaches, coach assignments, and coaching logs, it is challenging to build a coaching program.
- An agency needs systems in place to make the program become part of the organization, to include but not limited to a policy, an organizational home, a leadership champion, and other support.
- Funding is not likely to be dedicated for coaching programs because it is not a formal requirement. A business case needs to be made for funding (see Chapter 2).

- Coaching activities should be aligned to the agency mission and existing activities to gain credibility and sustainability.
- One barrier to success includes a persistent attitude that coaching is for remedial use and not understanding of what it is.
- There is no one best place for coaching to be housed, though the realm of leadership development seems to be a good fit.
- While it takes a strong personality and committed individual with a vision to start a program, an agency needs systems in place to make the program become part of the organization, including but not limited to a policy, an organizational home, a leadership champion, and other support.

Key Questions

- What challenges are you experiencing?
- What mitigations can you put in place?
- How can you obtain support from other departments in your agency to be successful?
- Who else from outside of your organization can you call on for assistance?

Leveraging Predictors of Success

4

> You have to act and plan for famine even when there's a feast.
>
> Cheri Allen

Thus far, we have discussed the beginning of coaching in the federal government and how coaching programs emerged in pockets across government. Many of these independent programs did not survive once champions and leaders moved on and the agency's priorities changed. Over time, however, things began to change allowing more coaching programs to emerge, like a slow rain shower, a drizzle that created puddles at first, then as the rain continued, formed pools. Eventually, the water level rose, and streams appeared. We believe the success of coaching in the federal government is demonstrated by the *lakes and tributaries* of coaching programs we see now and further evidenced by the fact that we constantly receive calls from government representatives asking how to establish a successful coaching program at their agencies.

What is a predictor of success for a coaching program? Before we answer this question, we need to define what we mean by *success*. In our interviews, we discovered that whether a program is continuously funded does not define its success. In the federal government, the priorities of leadership determine program funding, and leadership is constantly changing. An agency could have an award-winning program, and funding could still be unceremoniously eliminated without warning or apparent cause. We define success by the existence of policies that define leadership and employee development and how often the word "coaching" is connected to employee development

DOI: 10.4324/9781003218937-4

conversations. Success is the lake that has formed and coaching programs that continue to exist despite changing agency priorities. Continued success for coaching in the federal government is that the lake and tributaries continue to be refreshed and renewed.

If success is *the lake and tributaries themselves*, what provides the drops of rain that have the potential to refresh and renew? We believe there were several predictors of success that produced the rain for the most successful of programs. Program managers interested in launching or growing a coaching program or any program in the federal government must pay close attention to our claim that these were and continue to be predictors of success.

In the remainder of this chapter, we detail stories illustrating qualities successful coaching programs have in common:

- sponsorship
- coaching aligned to leadership programs
- right people, right place
- willing force of volunteers
- dedicated funding
- marketing
- collaborators

Sponsorship

Sponsorship at the highest level is crucial to any program. The most successful coaching programs in the federal government had sponsorship and support at the top levels of the organization. When a senior leader promoted a coaching program, subordinates quickly bought into the program and worked to make it successful.

When DIA lost two senior champions and advocates in 2019 and 2020, Dr. T. Fitzsimmons found herself in the position of needing to identify another champion for the program. When the new director arrived, she leveraged her contacts to obtain an introduction. Consequently, the new DIA Director was made a little more aware of the coaching program; he made a verbal endorsement at an agency-wide town hall event. This one mention from the new director could then be quoted in short articles and announcements, which, in turn, brought needed attention to the program.

Another example of the power of a senior leader's voice was at the beginning of the DAU Coaching Program. In his interview, R. Hansen talked about how John Young (J. Young), the Undersecretary of Defense for Acquisition and

Technology in 2007, was enthusiastic about his own coaching experience with Robert Hargrove. He arranged for funding to start coaching at DAU.

Prosci (2021) has researched change management best practices for more than 20 years and each year publishes *Best Practices in Change Management*. One of their seven best practices is to "mobilize active and visible executive sponsorship." Having a positive leader who actively guides the organization through change was cited four times more frequently than the next contributor to change success in this research. Strong sponsors:

- support change by giving consistent attention to the change and the need for change management
- champion change by leading and motivating others in the organization
- make effective and influential decisions regarding the change, including aligning priorities among other leaders in the organization
- influence peers to maintain buy-in and participate in a coalition of sponsorship

Undersecretary J. Young was one such sponsor for DAU, Richard Herrick (R. Herrick) was another such sponsor for DIA. He personally invited senior executives to participate in the first cohort and communicated with them as they progressed through the coach training program. He made every effort to communicate the power of coaching to the senior executive cadre at DIA. R. Herrick made coaching an organizational priority for his division and he recruited Dr. T. Fitzsimmons and Cynthia Covington (C. Covington) to create and manage the coaching program. He used his networking skills to gather buy-in for the DIA Coaching Program.

From our interviews, we collected best practices for finding a senior executive sponsor.

- Reach out to senior executives and ask them to provide a testimonial about their coaching experiences. Would they be willing to be interviewed?
- Create a presentation on the benefits of a coaching culture and ask permission to share it at the highest level.
- Offer shorter training sessions to the senior members on coaching skills if they are not available to participate in a full coach training program.
- If senior executives and managers have no coaching experience, offer to coach them on a provisional basis. If they find value in the service, they may be willing to agree to tell others about their positive experience.
- Have sponsors from another agency meet with executives from your agency and share how coaching has helped.

Coaching Aligned to Leadership Development Programs

In several of the early programs, we learned the coupling of coaching with leadership development was successful. The cost of qualified coaches, whether bought or internally developed, was seen as a logical addition and enhancement to the primary mission of leadership development.

Historically, federal agencies used contractors to deliver coaching services to the most senior employees attending leadership development programs. Many agencies still do this and with good reason. An external coach will be more objective when talking with a senior leader, who will feel psychologically safer knowing their coach is not an agency employee and internal to the organization (Ayuzawa, 2021). Also, research shows that leadership development instruction, when coupled with coaching, increases transfer of learning by 88 percent (Olivero, et al., 1997).

Since the 1990s, federal agencies provided coaching in leadership development programs to follow up a 360-degree assessment. Typically, assessment feedback was interpreted by a qualified debriefer, followed by a few hours from a certified coach, who may or may not have been the debriefer. Ideally, the coach's job was to work with the senior leader on areas identified in the assessment feedback for further development or exploration. This particular pattern of assessment, debrief, and coaching remains popular. As more agencies recognized the value of coaching, they brought coaching into leadership development programs. One way to do this, they realized, was to have internal coaches, which they reasoned would be cost effective.

Right People, Right Place

The right people in the right place included both great sponsors already mentioned and program managers and leaders who were instrumental to the program. These employees did something beyond their job descriptions and moved forward coaching in the federal government. We mentioned some of them in Chapter 1. Here, we will highlight several more.

Laticia Little

Laticia Little (L. Little) was instrumental in the success of the regional coaching program within Government Service Agency (GSA) Public

Building Service. She had worked as a civil servant for the Department of the Air Force and majored in marketing. Her colleagues and friends noticed she was good with people and suggested she pursue coaching, which she did in an unaccredited program. The Leadership Development program was in the Chief of Staff's office, where L. Little was also assigned. L. Little's boss noticed her talent and passion, suggested she start a coaching program for their division, and paid her tuition to attend an ICF-accredited program. In addition to offering coaching as part of the Leadership Development program, coaching became a regular offering to all GS-13s and above. L. Little attributed her success to a few key factors.

- **Placement of the program in the Chief of Staff's office**. This gave her clout in the field; other GSA employees saw Leticia as a representative from the Chief of Staff's office.
- **Her unique background and diverse skills**. Some of these included a background in Lean Six Sigma and marketing. She brought all of these to team coaching, which she also claimed was the future of coaching in the government.
- **Her highly successful marketing campaign**. She wrote many articles and literally ran a marketing campaign to promote coaching. She stated that "I shook hands and kissed babies" all over the agency. She visited every directorate. She stopped people in the hallway to ask how things were and eventually turned the conversation to coaching.

L. Little was the right person in the right place at the right time at GSA. In her interview, we felt her passion and enthusiasm and were particularly impressed how she put her experience and creativity to great use and never missed an opportunity to market the coaching program. She went from office to office speaking about the positive effects of coaching to anyone who would listen.

Julie Brill and Cassandra Brennand

As we discussed in Chapter 1, J. Brill, Director of Leadership Development and Executive, and C. Brennand, Program Manager of Leadership Development, were a pair of OPM employees in the right place at the right time. They identified the growing interest in coaching, surveyed private industry, and created a strategy to start a coaching program in the federal government without funding. They worked tirelessly to speak to the right people and bring others together.

Getting from the Bar to the Boardroom

Everyone is a salesperson. Whether you want to admit it or not, there is a point where you have to persuade an individual or group to change their current course of action in favor of a new one. This book is a sales guide, but more importantly, it is a guide on how to transition into the professional world and how to avoid the many pitfalls that have claimed countless victims.

Drawn from his successful career in corporate sales and client services, Doug Gentilcore shares his firsthand experiences and knowledge for developing a promising business career. In this innovative book, the author explains why any business professional, whether in sales or not, will at some point have to persuade an individual or group to change their current course of action in favor of a new one. Told via a clever and engaging narrative, this book delivers 25 proven skills for relationship building, networking, negotiating, business deal-making, and complex sales that business professionals can incorporate into their own work style. These include:

- Have Your Credentials at the Door
- If You Don't Have a "Big" Friend, Make One
- Bar Stool Selling
- You're Going to Get Shot Down, Deal with It
- Never, Ever Turn Down a Free Drink
- Know When It's "That Time"

Getting from the Bar to the Boardroom

25 Proven Sales Techniques for Relationship Building, Networking, Negotiating, and Dealmaking

Doug Gentilcore

Routledge
Taylor & Francis Group

A PRODUCTIVITY PRESS BOOK

First published 2023
by Routledge
605 Third Avenue, New York, NY 10158

and by Routledge
4 Park Square, Milton Park, Abingdon, Oxon, OX14 4RN

Routledge is an imprint of the Taylor & Francis Group, an informa business

© 2023 Doug Gentilcore

The right of Doug Gentilcore to be identified as author of this work has been asserted by him in accordance with sections 77 and 78 of the Copyright, Designs and Patents Act 1988.

ISBN: 9781032110639 (hbk)
ISBN: 9781032110622 (pbk)
ISBN: 9781003218258 (ebk)

DOI: 10.4324/9781003218258

Typeset in Cobol
by Deanta Global Publishing Services, Chennai, India

Contents

Preface

Far too often "sales" is given a negative connotation, and that drives me up a wall! Selling is essential for everyone and the ability to sell is something that is required in many areas of life. That being said, the will to sell varies, and I believe each and every one of us has the experience and skillset to successfully influence and persuade others. The lessons to follow are less of an instruction manual than they are a guide to help take what you have experienced in various social settings and apply them to your career. What you learn here will certainly help you in the business world; it will also apply to your personal life, especially your relationships and network development.

A wise man once told me, "Learn as much as you possibly can about your position and market." Of course, he meant learn your products and the sales model that my employer at the time had been inundating me with. But what he also meant was to embrace your position and the people you work around, understand their motivations and fears, and speak to both. Please heed these words from my very successful friend. The focus of this book is to help you maneuver between these lines, but without a solid knowledge base about your market, product, economic structures, and competition, you will not see the results you are hoping for after reading this type of guide.

I have sat through what has seemed like endless seminars and sales training exercises from various authors and thought, "I can't believe they are paying this character thousands or even hundreds of thousands of dollars for this stuff. It is common sense!" Some were very formal, opening, body, and close. Others were more democratic. Make sure you ask the customer a probing question, which depending on the salesperson wasn't a question at all, but more of an annoying tease. Some wanted us to give the customer a sort of colonoscopy, breaking down key decision-makers, gatekeepers, and leadership personnel, allowing us to develop a plan of attack. If you can just get all the questions on this worksheet completed, you will close the deal! All of these models had their merits and resulted in various levels of success and paperwork, but again, no real winners in my opinion. I then sought out the classics—Dale Carnegie, Sun Tzu, and a list of many others who were interesting but never really knocked my socks off; it became obvious that none of these people knew what the hell they were talking about! I got my job done and then some without these clowns; they were just giving my manager a reason to give me more busy work. It felt like a gigantic waste of time and resources. I thought, "the secret to my success is me; I am obviously built differently."

I know now that I was young and foolish, overconfident at best, and more likely arrogant. A few more years of this attitude and a tremendous amount of training and selling later, it finally hit me. The reason my employers had hired these individuals to train and speak to me, and the reason why I had been reading all of these books recommended to me, was that they had come up with a way to speak to their success in their own words. At this point, I had worked for three organizations in ten years, one small and two very large. I was 32 years old, married with a 20-month-old son, and I had enjoyed a fair amount of success. I had been given a number of promotions and blew out some sales numbers. By no means did I love my job, but I was making a good living, especially for a guy who had spent a little too much time in a bar/fraternity house/strange person's couch in his younger years. Life was pretty good, but I thought that I could do more with my professional life. So, over the course of a year or so, I looked at opening my own business, but I didn't have enough money or any great ideas. At that point in my career, I didn't think I was the idea guy, I was the give it to me and I will sell this thing to anyone guy. I looked for new jobs, but it was the same story but a different chapter, and I really couldn't go through another sales model and organizational structure.

So, what is a guy in his early thirties with a family he loves supposed to do? Should I branch out on my own, putting all of us at risk? Should I just suck it up and stick with what I was doing, so I could buy my family nice things, coach my son in the sports of his choosing, and maybe play some golf in the afternoon? Neither of these were horrible options by any means, so what was I to do? I decided I would write a book for young professionals getting started or established professionals looking to pull it all together. It all started on a long car ride returning home to Annapolis, MD, after a business trip to Roanoke, VA. I had always been a vigilant note taker, and possessed notebooks upon notebooks of customer facts, key learnings, and sales processes for deals won and lost. I could easily organize all this information into a book people would buy, right? Nine years and a global pandemic later, I can tell you one thing for sure: writing a book has been anything but easy.

C. Brennand's support also made the initial cohorts happen. In 2013 and 2014, A. Myers and C. Brennand spent hours planning and designing the program. It cannot be overstated that C. Brennand's role in the first three offerings of FICTP was immeasurable in terms of impact. She was the face of FCN and FICTP, which allowed A. Myers to focus on the design and implementation of the program and to work with the mentor coaches. When C. Brennand left the federal service, Elizabeth Winters took over as the program manager of FCN and FICTP, kept the program alive, and facilitated the transition from in-person to 100 percent virtual.

J. Brill and C. Brennand were the right people at the right time for all of this to happen. We are certain none of these actions were written in either of their job descriptions. They each had unique passion, vision, and belief that coaching was worth the effort.

Ruth Britt and Other Influential Voices

There were many voices in the initial design of FICTP. While having diversity of ideas and coaching philosophies was a strength, it was not without challenges and conflicts. There were competing philosophical approaches to coaching and the best way to develop new coaches. These philosophical conflicts were polarities that needed to be managed, not resolved. Among the many philosophical polarities were ontological and transactional approaches (otherwise known as coaching the who and coaching to solve the problem). Included in this creative tension was a focus on coaches as instruments (coaches working on themselves) and coaches managing conversations. This also created a conflict about how to train new coaches. In addition, it was virtually impossible to design training by a committee of 30 or more. Building a consensus was virtually impossible. It seemed at times that all was lost in terms of the "big hairy audacious goal."

Fortunately, some faculty/mentor coaches prevailed and did the work required to develop a cohesive course.

Ruth Britt (R. Britt) from Transportation Safety Administration (TSA), filled a void as a Director of Training. She applied her instruction design and project management experience to pull all of the course material together to offer a cohesive course. R. Britt initiated and implemented the first individual agency offering of FICTP at TSA. She took that experience and brought back lessons learned to FICTP and documented the instructional materials to share with other agencies. She pivoted when COVID necessitated the transfer of FICTP to a virtual offering and redesigned the course again to make it experiential and interactive in the virtual environment.

Dr. Theodora Fitzsimmons

In 2018, Dr. T. Fitzsimmons was on a rotational assignment in the Office of the Under Secretary of Defense for Intelligence (OUSDI) and in her role she promoted a Community of Practice with program managers, who began exchanging ideas about how to promote coaching across the community. At OUSDI, Dr. Fitzsimmons met C. Brennand from OPM and learned about FCN and CLOC. Through C. Brennand, Dr. T. Fitzsimmons learned about the stalled efforts at OPM to create policy to govern coaching. C. Brennand connected her with others who were willing to collaborate and gave counsel that OPM could not develop a policy but might accept a Guidelines for Coaching document. The group developed a 32-page document that included what the committee thought would be important for any agency wanting to establish a coaching program, but it did not get through the OPM guidance process. After more discussion and deliberation, C. Brennand and Dr. T. Fitzsimmons adapted the guidance document into a two-page memo. Again, the memo was slow to get through the OPM guidance process. C. Brennand left OPM, and Dr. T. Fitzsimmons persisted in getting this memo published. She asked J. Brill if she could periodically check on the progress.

Then, an opportunity presented itself. In 2018, Dr. T. Fitzsimmons was invited to Department of Defense Headquarters where they would be discussing the future of coaching and where Dr. Jeff T.H. Pon, Director of OPM, would be guest speaker. Dr. Pon was inspiring in his support of coaching. Everyone was riveted by his supportive words. At the end of his talk, he asked the audience of about 40 participants, "What can I do for you to help you further your cause?" Dr. T. Fitzsimmons did not hesitate. She said, "Sir, respectfully I would ask that you sign a memo or policy from the OPM level stating that coaching is a legitimate activity in the federal government and can be done on government time." Dr. Pon looked at J. Brill, who was also attending the meeting, and said, "Make it so."

Dr. T. Fitzsimmons' passion and belief in coaching is a story of perseverance. Although she has done a lot for coaching for DIA and FICTP, she considers this the single most important act she did for coaching in the federal government. The evidence of the significance is in the number of times we have seen the memo referenced in the government space for those who are interested in moving forward with coaching.

What can an organization do to identify the best candidates to be coaching program managers? A qualified, talented, and energetic program manager will make all of the difference to the success of the coaching program. We identified similar qualities in more than 40 program leads we interviewed.

- They believe in coaching and its effectiveness in making a difference.
- They are coaches themselves or are highly interested in becoming a coach.
- They are excellent at networking, or they are already very well connected.
- They are experienced in program management.
- They are very resourceful.
- They are resilient.

Willing Force of Volunteers

Building an internal coaching cadre in the federal government created a wonderful predictor of success: a willing force of motivated volunteers. The internal coaches emerging across the federal government will become the ambassadors for coaching and the force to remove barriers to success. Coaches know and believe they have the *calling* to help people, especially coaches in the federal government who are drawn to careers of public service. Finally, they also volunteer to accumulate coaching hours for credentialing purposes and to continue to grow and learn as a coach. Examples of this type of volunteering in other areas include mentor programs, conflict mediation, and the Combined Federal Campaign. Here are three examples of volunteerism in federal coaching.

A. Myers volunteers his time to serve as Director of FICTP, planning and managing FICTP around the duties of his full-time job based on the permission of his supervisor. In fact, FICTP is entirely run by volunteers, a group of dedicated internal coaches who serve as faculty, mentors, support coaches, and coaches.

At DIA, coaches willingly sign up to provide at least one hour of coaching (and more if the client continues), in the DIA Leadership Development Program. Their dedication and service orientation is apparent to Dr. T. Fitzsimmons, who observed coaches conducting sessions all hours of the day and night to support leadership development participants located across the globe. These coaches always check in at the session's conclusion and share positive attitudes and excited comments. "Just finished with a great client. Thanks for the opportunity!"

M. Dougherty has witnessed coaches from around the federal government volunteer to coach and support coach trainings. She believes there are two main drivers for employees to give their discretionary time to coaching.

1. **To connect with other coaches to continue their growth**. As members of the coaching cadre, they are part of a community of like-minded colleagues.
2. **To have a sense of purpose and accomplishment**. Several long-term employees have shared that becoming a coach renewed their sense of giving back, which initially brought them to government service.

At some agencies, the process to become an internal coach is very competitive because the agency invests in a small number of employees and pays the tuition for the coach training. In exchange, the employee makes a commitment to coach a significant number of hours (e.g. 100 hours per year), with the agreement of their supervisor of record.

At DIA, the required number of hours stated in the policy is 24 hours of coaching per year and attendance at three learning events, including at least one hour of ethics training. What happened over the first five years of the program is that some of the coaches coached the minimum number of hours, some coached many, many more hours, and some were not able to coach even the minimum. From the program perspective, these were all considered successful results because a coaching culture was still emerging where those who were learning coaching skills were becoming better leaders and had more productive conversations with their direct reports, peers, and managers.

Dedicated Funding

The program's trained coaches will naturally leave the organization in time, making the continued training of coaches paramount to the continuation and sustainability of the coaching program. At DIA, coaches left the program for various reasons: new job, retirement, they are too busy to coach, or they lose interest in coaching. A steady stream of new coaches keeps the program vibrant.

Initial and ongoing training of the coaching cadre requires dedicated funding. To get dedicated funding for the coaching program, we recommend creating a business case, discussed in Chapter 2.

Marketing

To be honest, few interviewees lauded their successes with marketing. However, L. Little's unique story of marketing success made us call marketing out as a predictor of success. This would be true especially in a federal agency where the changing agenda of leadership and the priorities of the day prevail, and coaching can be forgotten. Marketing can bring awareness of the availability and opportunities of coaching.

Although program marketing may seem easy to conduct, L. Little's background in marketing is a rare attribute of a coaching program manager. People with training, education, or coaching backgrounds do not necessarily have the knowledge to craft and execute a marketing plan.

One interviewee shared that their biggest challenge was convincing agency personnel to use available coaching resources. At this agency, the program was used so infrequently by staff that some coaches reached out to other agencies and offered their coaching services. This program could have used a marketing plan. Marketing is important and should also be planned up front. Use the graphics and/or marketing departments. Programs that are heard about get attention.

Collaborators

> As the lakes of coaching rise in the federal government, other agencies may be willing to collaborate and support your agency's coaching program.

Federal agencies are established for different public needs. However, human resources, training, and fundamental functions are common to all government agencies. It makes sense that members of one agency who perform a function may seek to collaborate with a counterpart at another agency. We have seen such collaboration for coaching across government agencies and we see this as an element needed for success. For example, a successful collaboration between L. Feingold, Dr. S. Stein, E. Bovaird, and others resulted in the Government-wide Coaching Consortium, a grassroots special interest group devoted to coaching in government who eventually approached OPM for assistance.

Another example of interagency collaboration occurred between TEI and Internal Revenue Service (IRS) to deliver a version of FICTP. They determined what would work best for both organizations' workforces, considered each program's constraints, and successfully delivered two cohorts of their adapted FICTP, adding 100 coaches to the federal coaching cadre as of this writing.

TEI built a relationship with ICF by providing quarterly coach coffees to engage their coaching cadre and other ICF coaches and with FCN by establishing quarterly training meetings for coaching program managers across government.

From 2018 to 2022, Dr. T. Fitzsimmons collaborated with DCPAS on behalf of DoD, participating in a coaching working group with participants from many different agencies. Jim Buchman, CLO, organized the volunteer working group into committees to collaborate on developing four pillars: policy, advice and consult, operations, and training.

In our interviews, we noted that recent collaboration demonstrates as much dedication and passion for coaching as collaborations among the pioneers of coaching.

Title: The Space Force Coaching Program

The Space Force Coaching Program

While meeting with many of the pioneers, and early adopters of coaching in the government space, we expected to find vision and passion, and we found it in abundance. What we were not expecting was the enthusiastic dedication of the newest coaching program managers who we met along the way. None were more excited about coaching and how it can positively impact their agency's culture and transform the lives of individual employees than Adam Edwards of the United States Space Force (USSF).

As a former Air Force Academy athlete, Air Force officer, and a person of strong faith and convictions, A. Edwards has the life experiences and personality to bring forth a compelling vision to a new endeavor. He developed a vision for the possibility of creating a coaching culture within the newly established military service from a series of compelling conversations with key leaders in the Space Force, Rodney Bullard, the CEO of Chick-Fil-A charitable division, and other influencers such as Mark Batterson, the author of Chasing the Lion, who all inspired him to make something happen at the Space Force. He got his own official training in coaching with a TEI/IRS offering of the FICTP. This experience, plus his strong sense of purpose and fearless determination to have bold conversations, convinced him that coaching was the right modality for the impact he wanted to make. He could clearly see coaching creating the environment for teams to be successful, and where individuals can make a strong contribution to the teams to which they belong. A. Edwards compared Space Force to NASA when it was a new organization in the 1960s, where curiosity, innovation, and risk taking were the life force of the Agency. A. Edwards believed coaching is one thing that would provide a "psychologically safe" workplace that encourages bold conversations, allow employees to "fail forward," and be a culture of non-reprisal for speaking up, or failing.

The insistence of A. Edwards to have courageous and compelling conversations with various leaders throughout the Force, even reaching out to senior leaders directly, led to the design of the Space Force Coaching Program in the Fall of 2021. The program started with the full support of the Space Force senior leadership, which we recognized in this book as one of the key factors for successful coaching programs.

A. Edwards talked about aligning the program with the values and commitment in the USSF aspirational vision document, "Guardian Ideal." He designed the Coaching Program to align with the elements of development, placement, evaluation, and feedback, all contributing to Space Force's desired culture. The vision is to have 20–35 internal coaches in each of three Space Force Commands, in addition to using external coaches to support the notion that everyone who wants a coach has access to a coach, regardless of rank or grade level. The internal coach in each Command would provide coaching to Guardians in a different command to maintain confidentiality. In the meantime, support and resources were sought for the coaching program to solicit contracting options to provide coaching to mid-tier and senior leaders in the Space Force. Coaching licenses were purchased to provide coaching to leaders along with the internal coaches. During the 2021–2022 timeframe, 111 Guardians received four months of one-on-one coaching with incredible feedback.

In addition to the Space Force external and internal coaches, they will also leverage other coaching resources within DOD, as well as the Federal Coaching Network. There is also a move afoot to train coaching skills for leaders in the NCO Academy Airman Leadership School and in the National Space and Strategic Studies program. This is the beginning of creating a coaching culture within the leadership ranks of the commissioned and noncommissioned officers and civilian force. Ultimately, the goal is to develop a psychologically safe place to work using a coaching approach and other modalities across the organization. Overall, coaching contributes to empowering a team of teams environment where cohesion and safety are valued. Part of the safe workplace, which according to Simon Sinek, "includes the use of empathy, which replaces judgment with curiosity."

A. Edwards is encouraged about the future impact of the USSF coaching program, and that it will truly make a difference and strengthen the overall culture of this new organization for mission success. He concluded his interview with this insightful message: "be kind, be curious, and be courageous."

Key Takeaways

*   The biggest predictor of success for a coaching program is having a senior sponsor, preferably one who has had a positive experience of having been coached. Reach out to senior executives in your agency and ask if they would be willing to provide a testimonial about their own coaching experiences.
*   When coaching is brought into the organization by connecting with the leadership development training and assessments, there is a good chance coaching will continue to be supported and will become part of the leadership development program.
*   In addition to having a senior sponsor, a strong coaching program manager is an excellent investment for the success of the program. Identify a strong program manager so you have the right person at the right time. This should be at a professional grade (GS-12 and above). Ideally, this person would be a coach or have an interest in becoming one.
*   Those who become coaches usually love it and want to offer their time to coach as well as support the learning and development of other coaches. Program managers can consider leveraging their talent to support their programs.
*   It is important to secure dedicated funding for the continuous training of new internal coaches. The coaches do eventually leave the organization for retirement or to get another job. Prepare the business case that shows potential ROI.
*   A full-on plan for marketing the availability of coaching is important to the success of the coaching program. Market the coaching program. If you do not possess marketing talent or experience, find someone who does.
*   Interagency collaboration may be an opportunity to do more with your coaching program than you can do alone.
*   Have a sponsor from another agency meet with some of your executives to share how coaching has helped his/her organization.
*   Seek opportunities to collaborate with program managers from other agencies.

Key Questions

- Who are your sponsors? How can you keep them engaged?
- Where is the best place for your program to be housed from? What would it take to have the program placed there?
- Who can help you with marketing your program?

References

Ayuzawa, K. (2021, October 18). How to nurture psychological safety in coaching. *Attuned.* https://www.attuned.ai/blog/how-to-nurture-psychological-safety-in-coaching

Olivero, G., Bane, D., & Kopelman, R. (1997, December). Executive coaching as a transfer of training tool: Effects on productivity in a public agency. *Public Personnel Management* 26(4), 461–469.

Prosci. (2021). Best practices in change management. *Thought Leadership*. Retrieved January 1, 2022, from https://www.prosci.com/hubfs/367443/2.downloads/thought-leadership/7-Best-Practices-in-Change-Management-TL.pdf?hsLang=en-us

Starting Off Intentionally

5

> Starting a coaching program was total experimentation and exploration. So it was both exhilarating, and sometimes a little scary.
>
> Lynne Feingold

As we explored coaching programs and reflected on our experiences, we noted key decisions that built strong foundations for the development of government coaching programs. Without acting intentionally to build strong foundations, programs were driven by individuals' beliefs in coaching rather than aligned to the agency's mission, embraced by its leadership, and supported by its resources. In this chapter, we streamlined a list of key questions to consider when creating a coaching program and answered each question, offering insights and examples.

- Who is the target audience for coaching?
- How many coaches will the program need?
- Should the program use internal or external coaches?
- What coaching methodologies will the program employ?
- What are the requirements for coaches?
- Will the program build or buy coach training?
- How will the program roll out and what is the communication strategy?
- What are the standards for coaching practice?
- How will the coaching program be resourced?
- In which department should the program reside?
- How will coaching align with other services and initiatives?

DOI: 10.4324/9781003218937-5

A key ingredient to making these decisions is taking the time to involve others and establishing the base of support necessary for long-term sustainability.

Who Is the Target Audience for Coaching?

Who in an agency receives coaching is not an obvious or simple decision and could determine the entire plan for the coaching program? What drives interest in establishing a coaching program at your agency?

- Making the agency's C-suite better leaders?
- Offering better incentives to employees and potential employees than the agency's competitors?
- Improving the agency's morale and culture?
- Providing better services to customers?
- Helping technical leaders transition to supervisors and managers?

In the 1990s and 2000s, similar to private industry, coaching programs in the federal government focused *only* on providing coaching to senior level leaders, usually executives. More and more federal agencies recognized the value of coaching for the development of leaders earlier in their careers.

Not only have federal agencies benefitted from investing in coaching to develop senior leaders and managers, studies also show that younger generations in the workforce value the investment organizations make in their training and career growth. In addition, coaching can be an indicator of increased employee engagement: 65 percent of employees from companies with strong coaching cultures rated themselves as highly engaged (ICF & HCI, 2014). Developing in-house coaching programs can benefit the agency's mission by expanding coaching to more audiences. This should be considered when identifying a program's audience.

In our interviews, we discovered agencies had adapted different resourcing models to meet the needs of their target audiences. From the inception of its award-winning Prism program, ITA provided coaching services to senior leaders and as part of its leadership development programs and continues to evolve and adapt to organizational needs and priorities as it pursues the vision of providing coaching to all employees around the world. Similarly, Environmental Protection Agency (EPA) and FCN provided full-service coaching upon request. Others, such as U.S. Immigrations and Customs Enforcement (ICE) and NASA, provided coaching to audiences in specific areas, such as leadership, career services, and conflict management. IRS accepted applications at specific times from specific audiences. In contrast, DIA and TEI were hybrid programs and used all the resourcing models.

Deciding your agency's target audience for coaching is essentially a strategic decision and comes down to determining what the program will do and how you will know that the program delivered it. Consider:

- What does the agency stand to gain (both costs and benefits) by offering coaching to certain individuals or groups?
- How will coaching affect performance? Attrition? Employee satisfaction?
- How will performance be measured? Are any of these measured now?

Performing this step up front will help you make the business case for resources and define the targets to track and measure over time that will determine the coaching program's ROI and benefit to the organization.

How Many Coaches Will the Program Need?

Calculating how many coaches the program requires to support the target audience is an important investment decision.

At DIA, leadership decided to budget training dollars to staff internal coaches to support 3,000 participants enrolled in the agency's leadership development program annually. The goal of DIA coach program managers was to train 500 coaches in the first five years and to continue to train 60 new coaches annually, to account for attrition. In their estimate for coach training, they also considered the number of hours coaches could dedicate, given the duties of their full-time jobs.

To determine their coaching needs, ITA's former Chief Learning Officer (CLO) Brian McNamara, along with the coaching program leads, developed a survey to gauge the level of organizational demand for coaching. The ITA identified the initial target audience and estimated a 20–30 percent participation rate. Given the level of demand and the number of coaches, the ITA batch-processed coaches in four- to six-month engagements that allowed it to effectively manage the demand while growing its coaching cadre.

The program initially began with a one-to-eight or one-to-ten coach-to-client ratio per year. As the program matured, it determined with its cadre of part-time coaches, that a one-to-six or one-to-eight coach-to-client ratio per year (i.e., one coach could support three to four clients every four to six months) was more manageable. They also planned for a 10–20 percent coach attrition rate (i.e., for every ten coaches, the program would lose one to two coaches annually). The ITA recruited new coaches every 6–12 months to ensure a sustainable cadre level. Ultimately, ITA's CLO and program leads determined that a coaching cadre that represented 1–2 percent of ITA's overall population was a healthy and sustainable level.

The demand-driven resource estimate formula and batch-processing of coachees used by ITA's program is a solid approach to realistically plan for the total number of coaches the program will need to support the target audience.

Another important factor to consider when determining coach resourcing is the timeframe over which you plan to provide coaching to satisfy the target audience(s) demand. For example, to gauge demand, ITA during its pilot phase, targeted approximately 500 employees. Roughly 160 expressed interest, or 32 percent. Given the supply of coaches and to manage the demand, ITA divided this audience in half (~80 coachees) to create two groups over four- to six-month phases. With its level of coaches (~10 at the time), ITA was able to provide coaching effectively and successfully to nearly all 160 staff within one year.

For sample planning purposes, if you expect to offer coaching to 1,000 employees annually and estimate that each coach can support up to eight clients a year (four coachees every six months), then your agency's program will need to invest in roughly 125 coaches. If each coach was able to support ten clients a year, then you would invest in 100 coaches.

Should the Program Use Internal or External Coaches?

Once the target audience is defined and the number of coaches necessary to accomplish the program's goals is determined, you need to consider how to staff the program's coaching cadre—with internal or external coaches, or a combination of both. Table 5.1 compares different aspects to consider for selecting internal and external coaches.

External coaches are experts, and partnering with them makes sense, particularly because employees in coach training programs require time to develop their expertise, their full-time jobs permitting them to typically only coach part-time. Seasoned external coaches can also mentor internal coaches pursuing their PCC credential.

Based on our interviews, most federal agencies started their programs with external coaches. The TEI Coaching Program was an exception and early adopter of employing internal coaches. Once established, the program shifted to a hybrid model and used internal coaches for GS-14 and GS-15 employees and external coaches for executives. Other agencies use a hybrid model of both contracted and internal coaches: contracted coaches for senior

Table 5.1 Comparison of Internal and External Coaches

Internal Coaches	External Coaches
• Have knowledge of organizational culture, politics, and internal dynamics • Have increased availability and are easier to contact • Can more easily gather feedback for the organization • Can model behaviors for other managers • Are more responsive to organization's needs • Can coach further down the organization's hierarchy • Have greater awareness of the client's specific context • Successful managers can more easily gain the respect of their clients and build rapport • Can gather learning to support the organization • Benefit the organization through their development as both a coach and client • Strengthen the internal networks of the organization	• Have experience in a variety of organizations and possess credibility, particularly with senior leaders • Possess more objective and balanced views • Are more flexible resource • Operate independently of organizational structure • Have clearly defined roles with no additional responsibilities • Will not already know the client • Can offer more challenging perspectives and a wider range of ideas • Have experience in different political nuances • Can say the "unspeakable" • Offer safer spaces to discuss sensitive issues

leaders and internal coaches for junior and mid-level leaders. We recommend establishing a contract with an external company to provide coaching to senior executives.

Using external coaches for executives is considered a best practice so that executives are coached from completely outside the system.

Ironically, at DIA, with the coaching cadre numbers in the hundreds and many coaches themselves senior executives, the SES population (formerly the only population offered coaching) became the least served population. However, as internal coaches gained experience and earned credentials, some senior executives started to accept coaching from their peers.

If your agency is starting a coaching program, contact the workforce to determine if any employees possess coaching credentials and are interested in joining the program. You may find credentialed coaches willing to come forward, once they know the program is being established.

What Coaching Methodologies Will the Program Employ?

So far, we have described one-on-one coaching as if it is the only method of coaching, but there are many methods of coaching that could align to both the goals of your agency's program and its resource constraints. Information about different coaching methods is plentiful but outside the scope of this book. Table 5.2 lists different types of coaching methodologies.

Table 5.2 Methodologies of Coaching

Type of Coaching	Definition	Purpose
Group coaching	Two or more people receive coaching where the participants have a common interest, but they are not necessarily connected in any other way.	Excellent when the organization can benefit from having groups of leaders receive coaching on key focus areas that will benefit their leadership and offer the opportunity to expand a coaching way of being into the organization.
Team coaching	Coaching for an intact team that works together toward a common goal. Coaching focuses on group dynamics and team focus.	Improves the capabilities of the team to increase productivity and effectiveness.
Peer coaching	Two individuals who have a mutual agreement to be coached by the other. There is a formalized arrangement between the two to meet for a certain period.	Can be an inexpensive alternative to bringing in fully trained coaches.
Action learning	Action learning is not coaching, but a group process that invites open dialogue and conversation. Having the leader also be a coach can be beneficial to the group process.	Excellent alternative to paying for coaching, but you run the risk of the conversation becoming too contested.

What Are the Requirements for Coaches?

Whether your program uses internal or external coaches, coaches should be credentialed. If you contract with a company, you can require external coaches to have a credential. If your agency's program plans to have an internal cadre of coaches, you need to plan to buy or develop training that will lead to certified and credentialed coaches by carefully documenting the expectations for attaining and maintaining credentials.

- What will be the standards of accountability for the coaching performed?
- Will there be an established number of hours of coaching required per year?
- Will there be professional development requirements to complete per year?

The starting point is to set a standard for training. Many programs require coaches to have completed or be pursuing at least a 60-hour ICF-approved certificate program or similar coach training. We recommend program managers conduct short interviews with each prospective coach to describe the program, learn about the coach's training and experience, and assess if the coach would be a good fit. It is a good practice for prospective coaches to review written guidelines and agree to abide by the policies and practices of the coaching program. Coaches may be asked to:

- adhere to standard coaching practices and competencies
- maintain confidentiality and coaching ethics
- establish coaching agreements with each client
- avoid being drawn into mentor, consultant, or therapist roles
- maintain a client-focused approach that leads to clients achieving their overarching goals
- be responsive to requests by program staff and clients
- provide necessary assignment information such as hours met and number of sessions
- contact the program staff when assignments end so evaluations can be conducted
- connect with program staff for assistance involving ethical dilemmas or questionable behavior
- submit a biography that may be shared with clients
- engage in continuous learning opportunities (some programs require a number of hours of training per year)

The ITA Coaching Program has also developed specific eligibility criteria and an application process to maintain their high program standards. Applicants to the ITA Coaching Program must demonstrate the following qualifications:

- possess grade of GS-13 or higher, or foreign service equivalent of FS-03 or higher
- have worked at ITA for at least two years
- have been in current position for at least one year
- received an overall satisfactory performance rating of a level three or higher on their last appraisal
- have written supervisory approval
- be willing and able to make the 18-month time commitment (six months of training followed by 12 months of coaching service)
- complete a minimum of 120 hours of formal professional coach training
- provide at least 100 hours of coaching to a minimum of 10 clients the first year

The entrance requirements to the DIA Coaching Program and ICF-accredited training are similar to ITA's requirements with two additions. At DIA, coach applicants must also possess a grade of GS-12 or higher and be a full performance employee (no longer in a development stage). The applicant's supervisor is required to attest to the statements.

Applicants to the DIA Coaching Program:

- are in good standing and there have been no complaints made against them as a supervisor in the last two years
- have a performance appraisal score of "successful" or higher
- commit to perform 24 hours of coaching per year (as the mission permits) and to attend at least three learning events
- agree to maintain a log of both the coaching hours delivered and the learning events conducted

Coaches who meet the requirements to be awarded a coaching certificate from an external program must also meet these requirements annually to maintain the designation DIA Certified Coach.

> Use an application process and selection criteria that is fair and consistent. For example, the coaching program for USPTO used an impartial board to review coaching applications and redacted all personally identifying information from each application to reduce bias.

Will the Program Build or Buy Coach Training?

When considering whether to contract for external coaches, recruit internal coaches, or train employees to become certified coaches, in addition to ensuring that the training program is cost effective, program managers must evaluate the needs and expectations of their target audience. Table 5.3 compares criteria to consider when deciding whether to buy or build coach training.

As a coaching program evolves, so does the decision-making process for selecting training. Many programs initially buy training services to build a cadre with the ability to meet the clients' needs. Once the cadre is seasoned and coaches can teach and serve as mentors, there is a capacity to develop and support internal training to create new coaches at a lower cost.

How Will the Program Roll Out and What is the Communication Strategy?

An insight we had while conducting interviews was the recognition of the challenges coaching program managers often faced to secure qualified communications and marketing expertise.

Table 5.3 Buy or Build Coach Training?

What Is Your Objective?	Consider...	Buy or Build?
You want to develop enough coaches so that every employee in your agency has the option to have a coach.	Training employees to be coaches part time	• Buy an external program to conduct training. • Build an ICF-approved program. • Consider borrowing FICTP.
You want enough coaches for your leadership development programs.	Training employees to be coaches part time	• Buy an external program to conduct training. • Build an ICF-approved program. • Consider borrowing FICTP.
You need enough coaches to support your senior leaders or high-potential employees.	Using external coaches	• Contract with an external company to deliver coaching.

Just because one knows how to coach or even manage a program does not mean that one has the knowledge, skills, and abilities to know how to roll out a program, create a communications plan, and execute that plan.

As mentioned in Chapter 4, L. Little had a very successful approach for marketing the GSA Coaching Program. Promoting a positive message about the program is crucial.

How can you acquire these skills for the coaching program? Include a communications plan in the roll-out strategy. Every agency typically has a marketing and communications function—contact this office for support. If your department has the budget, consider contracting with a marketing and communications vendor. Also, consider offering a temporary assignment opportunity to an employee. When considering marketing strategies, think low cost, high impact.

- **Make a plan**. Brainstorm things you will do to market the program and draw up a marketing calendar.
- **Identify communications locations** (e.g., regular emails from the Chief of Staff, Office of Human Resources, the Director, etc.) and get permission to post recurring articles about coaching.
- **Offer free tips.** People respond to free tips. Offer information on leadership, management, and communications. Search the internet for sites that provide useful tips.
- **Create a brand** for the coaching program. Find out how your organization creates brands and logos and use these internal services. If unavailable, use an inexpensive online service.
- **Create pins for your coaches**. Create a pin with the program's logo. Pins are inexpensive and important marketing tools.
- **Create an electronic badge for your coaches' signature blocks**. Create a badge that signifies you are a certified coach. Figure 5.1 presents badges used to distinguish different coaching credentials at DIA.
- **Create attractive certificates** displaying the coaching program's logo.
- **Create bookmarks**. These are inexpensive and useful marketing tools. For example, one side of the bookmark could describe where to find a coach, the other could display useful tips.
- **Create free training aids**. Anything you can make that is educational and free is helpful marketing.
- **Report data to leadership.** Keep program data updated and ready to present. Put a reminder on your calendar to report program data, including:

- number of coaching sessions conducted
- success or high-impact coaching stories
- statistics from coach feedback surveys
- cost savings realized from using internal resources
- FEVS data where coaching is strongest

A solid marketing plan can make the difference between program success and failure.

What Are the Standards for the Coaching Practice?

Several associations define the parameters of the coaching profession. The federal government does not officially endorse any single organization, and agencies can choose to follow the standards of any professional coaching organization.

- Association for Coaching (AC)
- Association for Professional Executive Coaching and Supervision (APECS)
- Coaches and Mentors of South Africa (COMENSA)
- Center for Credentialing and Education (CCE)
- European Mentoring and Coaching Council (EMCC)
- International Coach Federation (ICF)
- Worldwide Association of Business Coaches (WABC)

Professional standards in coaching include both the competencies governing what a coach actually does and a code of ethics. Another standard required

Figure 5.1 DIA Coaching Credential Badges, Designed by Aimee Merchant

by ICF is the coaching agreement between the coach and the client, which defines coaching, roles and responsibilities of the coaching relationship, limits of confidentiality, and code of ethics.

Limits of Confidentiality Agreements and Federal Employees

Coaching agreements include confidentiality statements about what a coach will or will not disclose, unless required by law. However, coaches employed by federal agencies must inform their clients of the legal limits of confidentiality due to their employment status. Federal employees are required to report fraud, waste, abuse, and other inappropriate actions. If a federal client discloses information about reportable legal activities during a coaching session, the coach has an obligation to report the information to the appropriate agency authority. (Information about what to include in the confidentiality agreement is described in Chapter 7. Also, a sample coaching agreement is available in the Appendix 2.)

How Will the Coaching Program Be Resourced?

Identifying resources to fund and staff any program is essential—no money, no program. As mentioned earlier, making the business case is very important for the success of the program, including identifying the ROI for coaching. Chapter 2 details this process. At a minimum, plan to fund the following activities.

- **Program managers**. We recommend at least one full-time, dedicated staff member assigned to administer and manage the coaching program.
- **Coach training program**. If your agency's program plans to use internal coaches, it will need to offer training that meets credentialing standards.
- **Software**. A web-based software program will help manage data, provide information to the public, and allow coaches to log their hours.
- **Marketing**. A well-planned and funded marketing campaign will result in a very successful coaching program.

One of the early pioneers, C. Allen stated, "You have to act and plan for famine even when there's a feast." Many programs have had to be sustained by internal coaches when coaching staff have been pulled. Infrastructure should be designed to withstand canceled funding.

In Which Department Should the Coaching Program Reside?

During interviews, we learned that federal coaching programs were rarely organized into the same departments across agencies. There were some departments more likely to house coaching programs, each with advantages and disadvantages. As mentioned in Chapter 3, there is no natural home for coaching in the federal government. Your agency's coaching program may have no choice about where within the organization it resides; however, this decision could hugely impact the program's strategy and management and could create challenges for the program's success.

Human Resources

From our interviews, we learned that the advantage of organizing coaching programs in the HR department was that coaching services could be included as a standard benefit to employees.

The potential disadvantage to coaching programs organized in the HR department was the stigma associated with alignment to a non-mission essential department, which suggested that coaching was of lower importance to the agency's mission. Also, unless HR was responsible for the agency's talent training and development function, HR leadership was often unfamiliar with coaching and did not support the continued professional development of the coach cadre.

Training and Education

We found many coaching programs were organized within their agency's training department when coaching was associated with leadership development. Coaching programs with an internal coach cadre often benefited when organized in the training and education department because these department managers understood training program execution and supported the professional development of coaches. The department also had contracts with qualified training vendors or had established competencies that necessitated requirements for Continuing Education Units (CEU).

One disadvantage to placing the coaching program in training departments was the misalignment of mission. Training facilitators and program managers were not necessarily equipped to administer coaching services or appreciate the coaching function. Also, when budgets became tight, training programs were generally one of the first activities the agency defunded, thus jeopardizing funding for coaching.

At DIA, coaching resides in the training organization. Mentoring and all other programs that exist to support employees are in Human Resources (HR). The lack of natural avenues for communication creates barriers to the success of the program. As a result, more efforts need to be made by coaching program managers to be in sync with the HR program managers, who tend to forget about the coaching program as they interact with the workforce.

Chief of Staff

An interesting finding from our interviews was that coaching programs operating from the Chief of Staff's office gained automatic credibility because the Chief of Staff legitimized the importance of coaching to the agency's mission. These coaching programs also retained sponsorship at a higher level when integrated into the agency's leadership office.

L. Little attributed part of the GSA Coaching Program's success to its placement in the Chief of Staff's office. This gave the program clout because other GSA employees saw L. Little as a representative of the Chief of Staff's office.

Program Offices

In our interviews, we learned about coaching roles embedded in program offices at the Food and Drug Administration (FDA). The Office of Product Evaluation and Quality within the Center for Devices and Radiological Health created a role, Associate Director for Professional Development, with one assigned to every office. These public health specialists, who possessed training in coaching and consulting, were embedded with scientists, medical officers, and medical device reviewers. They coached, consulted, and advised employees on their careers, professional development, and leadership capabilities. Similarly, the FDA Foods organizations trained investigators/inspectors, compliance officers, and food safety scientists to be internal coaches within their respective programs. These coaches focused on applying coaching skills or a coach-like approach and systems thinking to food safety.

How Will Coaching Align with Other Services and Initiatives?

In our interviews, we learned that when incorporated with other organizational services, the value of coaching increased exponentially. We learned of several programs established by one person or a small group of energized coaches that unfortunately ended when those people moved on, because the program was not aligned to the broader context of the agency's mission and purpose. For these reasons, we recommend coaching be integrated with agency departments on a broad level.

We believe how well a coaching program integrates into the fabric of the agency is critical to its success. The stories we heard from pioneers convinced us integration created a layer of importance and visibility for coaching.

Integration can mean a few things. Coaching is *added* to an existing program and eventually becomes synonymous with that program or *connected* with other programs and essentially exists together under one umbrella. In our interviews, we heard about coaching integrating (both adding and connecting) into various programs, including:

- leadership development
- 360 assessments
- senior executive onboarding
- career development
- conflict coaching
- mentoring

In this section, we present our findings for each of these programs and how coaching was integrated.

Leadership Development

In the federal government, coaching has frequently been integrated with leadership development programs. This affiliation was often the reason coaching was initially introduced in federal agencies. Typically, when participants were given the opportunity to take a 360-degree peer feedback assessment as part of their leadership development class, they were also assigned a coach, who would debrief the assessment results and coach them for a certain number of hours.

When paired with leadership development programs, coaching enables learning. This approach is supported by research: when coupled with coaching, transfer of learning from training potentially increases by 88 percent (Olivero et al., 1997). Consider participants in a leadership development class, learning about a new model or concept. As they begin the coaching portion of their program, the model and their thoughts about it are fresh in their minds. As they work with their coach, they talk about how to apply the model in their jobs or to a current leadership challenge. These coaching conversations lead to better retention of the leadership model.

At DIA, leadership decided to offer a coach to every participant in the Officer Development Training Program, to increase opportunities to make learning stick. Participant feedback about this approach was excellent. DIA could offer this service because the program had a cadre of trained internal coaches. In the 1990s and 2000s, other federal agencies added coaching services to training programs: Tina Frizzell-Jenkins at NASA talked about coaches supporting learning and Jerusalem Howard (J. Howard), mentoring program manager at ICE in 2011, talked about using coaches to support leadership development programs.

360 Assessments

We found in interviews that using an assessment as a starting point for a coaching relationship *was very useful*, especially when clients specifically wanted feedback. Coaches partnered with certified assessors to support the 360 feedback debrief. When clients arrived at their coaching session with assessment in hand, the coach simply asked, "What did you learn from this assessment that you would like to explore in coaching?"

At ICE, J. Howard described how the program used coaches to support employees who took both the 360 and other assessments. He separated the assessments from leadership training. Once employees received their assessment debrief, they were entitled to more hours of coaching.

R. Hansen at DAU described a 360 assessment for senior staff reminiscent of a coaching approach popularized by executive leadership coach Marshall Goldsmith that started with interviewing everyone in the leader's work environment, including direct reports, peers, managers, and the leader.

This approach was part of DAU's six-step coaching process and was highly successful to help leaders gain new perspectives and identify goals. The program won the ICF DC Metro Prism Award and was given an honorable mention for ICF Global Prism Award.

Senior Executive Onboarding

Similar to 360-degree assessments, coaching naturally aligns to onboarding, particularly when offered to newly appointed senior executives. We heard of this scenario in early coaching programs with external coaches contracted to assist with onboarding new executives.

Career Development

Coaching naturally partners with career development programs. At DIA, career development officers advise and support employees to explore and pursue different career paths. If also trained as certified professional coaches, they could offer employees the benefit of coaching to explore life goals and career next steps. Clearly, career advising is not coaching, but when coaching is added to the career advisor skillset, it creates a powerful combination.

Conflict Coaching

In our interviews, we learned of coaching programs that emerged in Alternative Dispute Resolution (ADR) departments that delivered conflict coaching. Offering coaching to help employees focus on goals and growth rather than conflicts was thought to be a healthy and positive service. Although agencies initially supported adding regular coaching to ADR departments, when leadership's priorities changed, the programs were defunded. We believe that in time, partnerships between conflict management and coaching programs will become more common.

Mentoring Program

Mentoring and coaching are different services with different approaches. However, to many federal agencies, mentors and coaches appear very similar.

An informal definition of mentoring is advice given from someone with more experience. Mentors do not require training to mentor others. In our interviews, we learned that employees often sought help from a mentor, not understanding the differences between coaches and mentors, and were happy for the support of either. For this reason, we were not surprised that many coaching programs were offshoots of mentoring programs.

Key Takeaways

- **Who gets coaching**: The decision about who gets coaching in your organization is dependent on what you want to get from coaching. The outcome should include who gets coaching as part of the strategy.
- **How many coaches:** To determine the number of coaches required for the program, think about the number of clients that will be met and decide how many clients can one coach realistically support.
- **Internals versus externals**: Based on the objectives for the program, you will weigh the pros and cons of using internals, externals, or a combination.
- **Methodologies of coaching**: When planning the coaching program, consider the use of alternative methods of coaching, such as group, team, and peer coaching.
- **Requirements for becoming a coach**: The application process should be fair and consistent and should follow a standard. We recommend using an impartial review board for internal applicants to the agency's coaching training program.
- **Buy or build**: Consider the objectives of the program when making this decision. If you want to coach everyone in your agency, then training internal employees would be a good investment. If you want to provide coaching to senior leaders only, then you would be best advised to purchase external coaches.
- **Marketing the program**: If you do not have skill or experience in marketing, it is important that you find it elsewhere. It is crucial to keep a positive focus on the program at all times.
- **Resourcing**: When planning for resources, make sure you consider all aspects that may require funding, such as the training program, a web program for managing coach assignments, marketing, and managers to run the program.
- **Location of program**: Although you may not have a choice, the decision where your program is managed from can play a huge role in its success.

- **Alignment with other services**: Although one can start with a limited definition of coaching, when incorporated into other services in the organization, its value can increase exponentially.

Key Questions

- What will be a healthy process for decision making? What key stakeholders should be included?
- Which of the key questions do you believe are most critical for your program's success?

References

International Coaching Federation, & Human Capital Institute. (2014). *Building a coaching culture* [Report]. https://researchportal.coachfederation.org/Document/Pdf/1313.pdf

Olivero, G., Bane, D., & Kopelman, R. (1997, December). Executive coaching as a transfer of training tool: Effects on productivity in a public agency. *Public Personnel Management* 26(4), 461–469.

Sustaining a Vibrant Program   **6**

> When you've had an executive go through a coaching program and it was successful, they become your best advocate for coaching.
>
> Randy Bergquist

Sustaining newly established coaching programs is like tending freshly planted trees—both need water and care so their roots grow deep and they thrive. Sustainment of coaching programs must be carefully planned. In this chapter, we discuss considerations you need to make in order to ensure your program continues to thrive.

Continuously Acquire Senior Leader Support

At EPA, B. Weber's role as a director enabled her to put the coaching program in place and support it. Similarly, the coaching program at DIA was successfully implemented largely due to senior leader R. Herrick, who secured seed money for the pilot program. The coaching programs at both EPA and DIA had strong starts due to senior leader support; however, sustaining the programs depended on continuous senior leader support. New senior leaders

> Keep working to gain the support of senior leaders who remain in the organization.

DOI: 10.4324/9781003218937-6

replacing program champions may be unfamiliar with the coaching program, unaware of its successes and how it benefits the organization. With their new priorities and pressures, new leaders could easily dismiss coaching.

A smarter strategy, given how easily priorities change, is to steadily work to gain the support of senior leaders. At DIA, the coaching program continued to garner support because many senior leaders had trained as coaches and realized its value to the culture of the organization. When the original champions departed, program managers only needed to enlist the support of new champions.

As mentioned in Chapter 5, request and prominently post endorsements from seniors about the effectiveness of coaching and its value to the organization. Otherwise, you will constantly need to reach out to new senior leaders to request they actively support the coaching program.

Prepare for Your Next Request

> As the program manager, you need to tell your organization's story and network to maintain support for it. As pioneer C. Allen shares, "Build your strategy through relationships." Collaborate with key players in the coaching community to identify opportunities. Stay aligned with your agency to recognize areas of integration. Keep dreaming and always know where you need support and what you would request when talking to key leaders.

Maintain Engagement with Partners in the Organization

There are reasons to engage with other offices in the organization, some we have described in Chapter 5. These partnerships also become important for the continued life of the program. Partners remember how jointly held activities benefitted the workforce and they help to market your program. See Table 6.1 for ideas on alliances between coaching and other programs.

DIA's coaching and mentoring programs jointly conducted an event called "Speed Coaching and Mentoring." Program managers set up a large room with chairs and employees either signed up or dropped in on the event to experience both mentoring and coaching.

Table 6.1 Alliances Between Coaching and Other Programs

Mentoring	Offer joint activities Jointly market both programs
Ombudsman	Create handouts about coaching for the Ombudsman office
Equal Opportunity (EO)	Create handouts about coaching for the EO office
Employee Assistance	Create handouts about coaching for the Employee Assistance office, emphasizing the differences between coaching and the therapeutic work of psychologists
Alternate Dispute Resolution (ADR)	Partner with ADR on projects that help organizations move beyond a conflict and to a more positive future-focused direction
Employee Management Relations	Create handouts about coaching for the Employee Management Relations office
Office of General Counsel	Create handouts about coaching for the General Counsel's office
Office of Inspector General	Create handouts about coaching for the Inspector General's office
Career Development	Offer coaching to career development visitors interested in exploring what they want to do with their careers before getting specific career advice Develop a joint event with the Career Development office and with both coaches and career development officers

Table 6.1 lists possible alliances between coaching and other programs.

Take Care of the Coach Cadre

Most employees who become coaches are enthused and addicted to it. If the reader is a coach, you know what we are talking about. Coaches typically want to continue to learn, grow, and improve. The coaching program cannot just be about training new coaches and finding coaching assignments but must also provide avenues for growth to keep the existing coaching cadre engaged and enthusiastic.

When M. Dougherty became a coaching program manager, she realized that for the program to remain successful, she needed to attract more coaches.

Her strategy was to build a community where coaches wanted to belong. She implemented an annual survey to learn what coaches wanted from their community and held monthly meetings to build community and promote communication. Some monthly meetings offered continuing education workshops on coaching competencies and related topics. Other meetings delivered updates on program changes or important information from ICF. Meeting agendas included "open mic" time to encourage coaches to ask questions and share tools and ideas. M. Dougherty launched a monthly newsletter and established an online community of practice where coaches could celebrate successes, share resources and inspiration, and where training updates were posted. The coach training program evolved to meet the needs of their coaches and included mentor coaching and CEUs. The coaching program staff prided themselves in always returning coaches' calls and messages in a timely manner. They found that most of the time, coaches, especially new ones, simply wanted to share an idea or be coached on a situation they were experiencing.

Over five years, Dr. T. Fitzsimmons developed a robust community of practice for the coaching cadre at DIA and created an ICF-approved continuing coach education program that offered 120 possible options for credit. Each year, the program manager processed a proposal with ICF to be accredited for the following year. The training categories included advanced competency training, services, and special topics.

- **Advanced Competency Training**: 90-minute webinars on the ICF Coaching Competencies.
- **Services Series**: 60-minute webinars where other helping services presented their programs and answered questions. These events gave coaches an opportunity to become familiar with available helping services at DIA where they could comfortably refer clients as needed. These events were not about diagnosing problems, but about helping coaches recognize when clients presented situations outside the scope of coaching.
- **Special Topics**: Webinars on a multitude of topics of interest. Some of the titles: Polarities Coaching, Neuroscience, Tools in Coaching, Coaching Supervision.

For FICTP, Dr. T. Fitzsimmons and A. Myers developed ICF-approved mentor coaching training, with up to 24 hours of coach-specific training that was a requirement for all faculty, mentor coaches, and support coaches. The instruction included a deep dive into ICF competencies and listening and assessing recorded coaching demonstrations. Participants were required to assess a recording using a set of assessment criteria and receive feedback on their performance. This program enabled participants to take their coaching and their ability to help other coaches to a new level of competence.

If coaching program managers cannot offer training internally, they should identify other opportunities for coaches to earn CEUs. For example, ICF has a global network of chapters that offer continuous learning opportunities.

Keep Possible Focus on the Program

Based on our interviews with pioneers, we cannot overstate the importance of making the coaching program visible. The marketing plan must be in place early in the program's inception and communications conducted routinely.

As the program manager, your goal is to convince senior leaders that the coaching program is worth keeping by demonstrating with either ROI or ROE studies how the organization has benefited from funding coaching and why it should continue to do so. In Chapter 2, we explained that ROI studies are most useful if initiated when the coaching program is established. This data will make the case for the value of coaching to both those who appreciate it and who need to learn its worth.

Besides ROI and ROE studies, the program's marketing plan plays a crucial role in sustaining the program. A strong marketing plan keeps the program visible and creates a common reference to coaching for everyone in the organization, especially senior leaders.

Pioneers emphasized how a strong marketing strategy helped their coaching programs. R. Hansen of DAU said, "Talk about your program as often as you can. Then talk about it some more." The DAU Coaching Program is one of the most successful programs in the federal government. R. Bergquist, formerly of the Department of Justice, found that the program was best marketed by the coaching program graduates and their clients' testimonials. They were *disciples* of the coaching program and returned to their organizations modeling newly learned behaviors, sharing their positive experience, and garnering sponsorship for the program. In addition, testimonials from credible colleagues went a long way to earn support for coaching.

Preserve Standards for Coaching Practice

Sustaining standards for the coaching practice is also important for sustainability because they demonstrate the program's credibility.

In interviews, the most successful programs had clearly communicated coaching standards and ethical guidelines endorsed by a coaching association. When federal coaching programs do not adhere to this practice and do not maintain high standards of professionalism, the results can be disastrous.

In one interview, we learned that an agency's coaches, who were also counseling psychologists, were dismayed when some employees defined themselves as facilitators qualified to provide coaching and team interventions, without first validating their coaching credentials with the counseling center. The culture of this organization accepted the word of employees who stated that they were coaches, even without evidence. The counseling center combated this problem by publishing a list of coaches who had completed certification training and possessed professional coaching credentials.

Another organization created a credibility problem when they established an internal coach training program that was not accredited. The newly trained coaches were only allowed to coach employees at that organization. Over time, the professional development of these coaches suffered because the agency's unaccredited training program did not qualify them to coach at different federal organizations or participate as a coach mentor in FICTP.

For federal coaching programs to thrive, coach training programs must be accredited, and all coaches must possess or be working toward credentials from a recognized accrediting institution that demonstrates their knowledge of the profession and ethical standards of coaching. Federal coaching programs with credential requirements are more assured that coaching in their organizations is conducted correctly and compassionately, is not harming anyone, and is not attempting to deliver therapy.

Monitor Coaching Practices

Monitoring coaching activities is crucial to sustainability. What is important to monitor?

Adherence to ethics and effective coaching practices. Make coaching effectiveness surveys available to all coaching clients to complete at the end of their coaching engagement. In addition, program managers should make training on ethics available, support coaches through mentoring and supervision, and provide a place for coaches to seek guidance when they encounter an ethical dilemma.

Coaching delivery. Chapter 3 describes the importance of having a software system to track and manage coaching activities and collect business case data. This information also helps to evaluate coach performance, client satisfaction, and program effectiveness. Sample surveys are available in the Appendix 2.

> The coaching agreement encourages transparency and reduces the opportunities for misunderstandings.

Coaching agreements. We believe coaching agreements are crucial because they encourage transparency and reduce opportunities for misunderstandings. They are required by coaching professional associations, including ICF, and should be required for every coaching engagement. The coaching agreement forces the conversation between coach and client about what coaching is and is not, about confidentiality and the limits of confidentiality, about the code of ethics, and about roles and responsibilities. Here are two ways to ensure coaching agreements are established between your coaches and their clients.

1. Ask coaches to upload agreements to an online repository.
2. Include a question in your coaching effectiveness survey: "Did your coach review a coaching agreement with you in your first or second meeting?"

Dr. T. Fitzsimmons used the ICF Coaching Agreement template and researched government conduct rules and stated behavior guidelines applicable to DoD and DIA before drafting an agreement and submitting it for review to DIA's General Counsel. This agreement is used by all coaches at DIA.

Coach mentoring and supervision. This requires the presence of trained and experienced coaches capable of giving constructive feedback to other coaches about their coaching abilities. Dr. T. Fitzsimmons trained DIA's coaches to become coach mentors so that they could be available to review recordings of fellow coaches. She and C. Covington also completed training to become coaching supervisors, qualified to provide group and one-on-one supervision. At DIA, mentoring and supervision were encouraged but not required.

Try New Things

As coaching programs mature, they run the risk of becoming irrelevant if they do not remain current with the latest coach techniques and the needs of their organizations. As the program manager, how will you adapt the coaching program to best serve its audience?

Consider Team and Group Coaching

Coaching can only affect the number of employees reached. One answer to the continual request to do more with less resources is for coaching programs to introduce team and group coaching.

Team Coaching. A simple definition of a team is a group of people working together to accomplish a common mission or objective. Team coaching brings together individuals aligned around a shared goal. Some areas that teams may choose to explore are developing clear goals, improving team performance, collaborating generally or on a specific project, working through conflicts, and making decisions. A coach works with a team to help them move forward in a fashion that is designed and agreed upon by all.

> Some might think that team coaching is the same as team building. While team building is important, team coaching is about digging into the tough stuff to create tangible alignment and cohesive teams. Team coaching includes a blend of coaching, teaching, facilitation, mediation and positive psychology. It helps your leadership team lead as a consistent principal of the organization.
>
> (Lofgren, 2020, Team Coaching vs. Team Building)

Group Coaching. While similar to team coaching, group coaching is distinctive because it involves participants coming together around a common interest or topic while maintaining their individual goals. Their choices and future actions rarely affect others in the group, although there is power in their ability to support and hold group members accountable. Topics could include first-time supervisors, leading in uncertain times, or writing a book. The coach works with the group as they share insights and learn but they move forward as individuals benefiting from their own plans and actions.

Both options are a better use of resources, with one coach supporting multiple clients at the same time. They can also be more effective than one-on-one coaching.

> For clients, group coaching can be appealing as it involves a peer learning process. Some coaching clients prefer a collaborative group learning environment where they learn from the insights and contributions of peers, as they do from their own reflections. For clients who are more introverted, the peer learning process may feel "less on the spot" and provide more time for reflection and articulation of their insights. The "collective wisdom" created and explored is often identified as a key benefit.
>
> (Britton, 2021, Peer Learning Process)

There are plenty of resources on team and group coaching that program managers can explore. We recommend capturing stakeholders' insights and conducting a pilot for viability. If it goes well, you could expand into areas which involve training coaches, educating employees on the different options, and setting up related logistical processes.

Collaborate, Experiment, Adapt, and Take Risks

TEI is a leader in executive and senior leader development because its culture allows for experimenting and taking risks. The TEI Coaching Program benefited from this culture. In 2017, they implemented group coaching.

Joining efforts with other agencies is an excellent way to strengthen the coaching program and increase visibility. TEI partnered with USCIS to pilot on-demand coaching, a program that within 48 hours of a request, provided a coach to a client with a developing issue. The program used an amended agreement and scheduled on-call coaches who met with clients up to three times within a specified period. The pilot for this service was a success but TEI did not have the resources to sustain it.

DIA offered 10 percent of enrollments to its Coach Training and Certification program to employees from other organizations. The strategy was to build a cadre of external federal employee coaches who could also support DIA. Having the option to select a coach from another agency made some DIA clients more comfortable with receiving coaching from an internal coach.

The coaching program's training strategy must be adaptable and include continuing education for both new and experienced coaches that awards CEUs. It should include mentor coaching, which is necessary for coaches to maintain their credentials. It was also important to offer master coaching events for coaches with 200+ hours to keep these seasoned coaches engaged. Collaborating and sharing content across agencies enables quick growth and flexibility for all.

The coach training program at TEI offered an introductory series "So You Want to be a Coach?" for interested parties to explore coaching basics and to understand the challenges of coach training. Employees taking this series performed better in their certified coach training.

Expanding Your Portfolio

As an internal coaching program grows and as coaching becomes more recognized as a valuable skill set, coaching program managers of internal coaching programs may find themselves with the need to evaluate and consider expanding their offerings and products. Providing coaching to a specific population, either by buying external coaches or building internal ones, may not satisfy the needs of the organization. How else can these coaching program managers build capacity and value? See Appendix 3 for several additional kinds of programs that can be added to the portfolio of a coaching program.

Title: Coaching in the Department of the Army

Coaching in the Department of the Army

For every coaching program success story, there is a leader and visionary behind it. For the Department of the Army, that person was Lieutenant Colonel (LTC) Christine Baker. LTC Baker's coaching story started in 2019 when she was assigned to the Army Talent Management Task Force. She was told that she would be heading up "Career Coaching" for the Army. She didn't really know what coaching was yet, but she put her investigative skills to use. She found out that there had been coaching pilot programs that started in 2018 with Army Talent Management Task Force and the Office of Economic and Manpower Affairs. These pilot programs targeted junior-career officers who were given assessments for self-awareness and were also given the opportunity to explore different career interests and choices, with the assistance of Army resources or coaches (coaches provided by OPM's Contracted Credentialed Coaches). What got her attention right away was that given the choice of internal Army resources or the OPM coach, the participants chose the coach every time.

Tasked to create a program, LTC Baker needed more data before she could put a plan together. She reached out to Rice University and learned from their research; 35–40 percent of students offered coaching accepted. She decided to see if that would be the same for the Army. Her first action was to recommend a new pilot program for mid-tier officers newly promoted to the rank of Major. These officers would already be receiving assessments, so the difference would be to offer them the opportunity to get a professional coach. She wondered how many would accept the offer. There was 315 in the group and 111 accepted. The amount of positive feedback from those who received coaching was overwhelming. The feedback was so positive during the pilot, it was suggested that coaching be offered with the Command Assessment Program, which assesses an officer's readiness for command. The first pilot was not even over when this second request came in! With

760 Officers, the Army did not have the internal capacity of trained, certified, credentialled professional coaches to cover the requirement, even if only 35–40 percent accepted the offer. LTC Baker, however, was very resourceful. By this time, she had reached out to the government community of coaches and found where she could attain more coaches. She was able to get more coaches from the Army coaching program on the civilian side and from the Department of the Interior's Federal Consulting Group by utilizing a contract. The program was a resounding success. Over 2,000 had gone through the coaching program at the time of the interview, and more than 800 more were signed up for the coming year.

LTC Baker's plan was just beginning. She saw the next step for the Army's coaching program to be to work with Department of Defense and the Army Senior Leaders to create a policy around coaching. Again, she used her resourcefulness to find other examples of coaching policies to leverage.

In addition, the Army joined efforts with the Air Force to create an internal coaching cadre. This internal cadre would ultimately reduce the costs of contracting. At the time of the interview, 75 coaches had been trained, with 40 due to graduate that year.

Not everything came easy. A challenge was messaging what coaching is and what it isn't. The Army is uniquely adept at developing leadership skills and qualities in all employees. Mentorship is one of the leadership skill sets. The messaging around the distinctions between mentoring and coaching was extremely important. LTC Baker increased messaging about the power of coaching with memos, pamphlets, articles, PowerPoint presentations, and podcasts through the U.S. Army Association. One strategy LTC Baker promoted that would solidify the understanding of the importance of coaching is creating Army Coach designations. This was a very important development because it is part of the military culture and formalizes the role. The four levels of Army Coach designations include the demonstration of coaching competencies and experience. To receive the first-level designation, the Officer must have had at least 80 hours of coach-specific training. For the second level, they need to have had 100 hours or more of coaching experience (parallels the ACC credential). The third level would be the equivalent of the PCC, and the fourth would be the equivalent to the MCC level. Announcing the designation levels drew the interest of other Army

Officers who were already coaches. Six individuals came forward from both the Army Reserve and National Guard force, expressing interest in the new coaching designation. This would serve as a huge motivator to pursue coaching as a profession, develop leadership capability across the military, and legitimize coaching as a development mechanism.

LTC Baker herself also became a coach and her life plans and dreams were forever changed as well.

Key Takeaways

- The support of senior leaders cannot be overstated. It is best to cultivate relationships with senior leaders to support your program continuously.
- Maintaining partnerships with other programs in the organization helps to create a symbiotic, mutually beneficial alliance that supports the success of both programs. Engage with partners within the agency that offer other services to the workforce.
- Internal coaches greatly benefit from continuous learning opportunities that the coaching program provides. Take care of your coach cadre by offering them opportunities to learn and grow.
- Taking every opportunity to promote the availability and benefits of the coaching program helps to the long-term sustainability of the program. Keep a positive focus on the program by marketing the program and having ROI/ROE information at the ready.
- Coach training programs must be accredited, and all coaches must possess credentials (or be working toward them) from a recognized accrediting institution that demonstrates their knowledge of the profession and ethical standards of coaching.
- Coaching programs need to ensure that coaching delivery is done in a consistent way. One way to ensure this is to make sure that coaches continue to use standard practices such as coaching agreements, that they provide surveys to their clients, and that they continue to do coach mentoring and supervision.
- One way to keep the coach offering visible is to keep introducing new offerings, such as team coaching, peer coaching, and group coaching. Coaches will also be happy and engaged as they are exposed to learning new techniques.

Key Questions

- What will keep your program vibrant?
- Who can you network with to help find senior leader support?
- What other offices in your organization can you partner with to offer common events?
- What is the process for getting the coaching agreement legally approved in your organization?
- What platforms are available in your organization that you can leverage for your coaching program?
- What are the latest trends in the coaching field?

References

Britton, J. (2021, October 8). What are the benefits of group coaching? *The Coaching Tools Company.com.* https://www.thecoachingtoolscompany.com/group-coaching-benefits-coaches-clients-organizations-by-jennifer-britton/

Lofgren, J. (2020, September 16). How team coaching can help your executive team lead as one. *Forbes.* https://www.forbes.com/sites/forbescoachescouncil/2020/09/16/how-team-coaching-can-help-your-executive-team-lead-as-one/?sh=5af3dd111a1c

Establishing Good Governance

7

> Without a governance structure that includes policies, procedures, administrative processes, leadership, and accountability, a program will have limited to no long-term viability, sustainability, or success.
>
> Alan Lee Myers

Good governance promotes fair and positive behavior at all levels of organizations. In our interviews, we found that many coaching programs were started by individuals who understood the value of coaching but did not consider how coaching would be managed or integrated long-term. Therefore, few examples of good governance existed in early coaching programs, which had a long-term impact on the sustainability of coaching in the federal government. We recommend that organizations establish a governance structure before putting a coaching program in place and to publish policy for the program as soon as possible.

Levels of Governance

Governance in organizations includes the regulations, practices, and structures that enable transparent decision making and protect the interests of everyone. Policy is integral to the success of any federal program, providing legitimacy or top cover. OPM is the agency responsible for performance management in the federal government, and ideally would direct policy to govern coaching programs. As of 2022, the 2018 OPM Memo serves this

DOI: 10.4324/9781003218937-7

role for coaching; however, it is a memo and not federal policy. Regardless, we know the coaching community is happy to have it. For department-level agencies, the OPM Memo, as of this writing, is also the only official guidance governing coaching programs. For DoD agencies, in 2021, Dr. T. Fitzsimmons led a sub-committee to update DoD Instruction 1400.25, Volume 410, *DoD Civilian Personnel Management System: Training, Education, and Professional Development* to include a statement on coaching and to draft a chapter in one of five handbooks included with the instruction. Once completed, this updated policy will enable DoD agencies to develop internal policies to govern coaching.

We offer two case studies on creating governance for federal coaching programs: DIA and FICTP at OPM.

Creating Governance at DIA

Between 2016 and 2022, Dr. T. Fitzsimmons pioneered the development of governance for the DIA Coaching Program. DIA follows DoD standards, structure, and policy. The performance management policies cascade from OPM and DoD to DIA.

In 2016, Dr. T. Fitzsimmons, wanting to legitimize coaching at DIA and make it available to all employees, initiated the development of an agency-wide instruction, but was directed to create an administrative instruction that would be issued by the training department. Although this was better than no policy at all, because it was not among agency-level policies, DIA management could still contest it if they did not want the workforce to participate in coaching. For example, if a DIA employee asked to become a coach or seek coaching, the supervisor could easily say no because there was no mandate or policy to easily reference. The administrative instruction did a good job laying out the basic governance for coaching as it existed at the time.

With the publication of the 2018 OPM Memo, discussions about policies began to occur. For example, Defense Civilian Personnel Advisory Service (DCPAS) started to dialogue about coaching more seriously at the DoD level. DCPAS oversees human resources policies for over 900,000 government civilians and understands that policy will increase acceptance of coaching as a legitimate professional development practice.

With the new DoD Instruction and Handbook (under review), the environment will begin to change. It makes readdressing the need for policy at DIA easier to accomplish. Dr. T. Fitzsimmons submitted a draft of a DIA

Guide in 2022 as an addendum to the agency-wide training policy. This DIA Guide includes the specifics of the coaching program and would be accessible at the agency level.

Creating Governance at FICTP

FICTP also struggled with lack of policy and governance. The program exists because of an agreement from CLOC and the Leadership Program Office at OPM. Since 2014, FICTP has delivered ICF-accredited coach training and collaborated with other agencies to deliver off-shoot training programs without much guidance and a minimal amount of support. In 2018, recognizing that lack of governance created fragility and vulnerability for FICTP, A. Myers led efforts to create the FICTP Governance Board, composed of volunteer stakeholders and the FICTP Training Coordinator at OPM. In 2020, the board drafted a charter and submitted it for approval to OPM. The draft charter defines procedures for curriculum decisions, program accountability, and program execution.

The FICTP Governance Board is composed of senior coaches who have been instrumental in the program from its early years and continue to have an interest in its success. It is a volunteer role again and A. Myers chairs it. The board has the ability to ensure consistency of the program as it evolves and if A. Myers moves on. Some key decisions where the FICTP Governance Board were involved:

- when the COVID-19 pandemic forced the program to adapt to a virtual offering
- when new agencies requested to leverage program materials to deliver an iteration of their own
- when an agency wanted to pilot a 60-credit iteration of the program (versus 136-coach training hours)
- when ICF changed rules for the mentor coach qualifications and virtual course delivery

As of 2022, OPM has not responded to the board's charter, leaving FICTP without official governance, and making the future of FICTP vulnerable to changes in priorities of the OPM Leadership Program office. A. Myers and the unofficial governance board continue to meet to make decisions based on their willingness to discuss and come to consensus for the greater good of coaching in the federal government.

What to Include in Governance

The story of the FICTP Governance Board's charter models how to establish a governance board. We also researched the literature to find other recommendations.

According to Nicholas J. Price (2018), "good governance has nine major characteristics that set the tone and environment for all individuals to have a voice" (see subheading, What Constitutes Good Governance). These nine characteristics provide a good lens for program managers to look through when setting up governance and policies.

1. **Participation**. There should be a governance board consisting of a diverse group of people with varying skills, talents, abilities, experiences, and perspectives. Board members should be expected to participate in all board meetings and chairpersons should facilitate the meetings in a way that draws out the perspectives of all participants, to gain everyone's views.

2. **Consensus-oriented**. A board is expected to have differing opinions and perspectives. Encouraging debate and discussion is healthy and can lead to the best decisions that benefit the program.

3. **Accountability**. Board members need to hold themselves accountable to their stakeholders, employees, and the public. In the case of a coaching program, the governance board may need to be held accountable to the coaches, management, and the public.

4. **Transparency**. The governance board of a coaching program may be responsible for how coaches are selected to participate in the training program. Transparency of the records and processes engenders trust among the stakeholders and ensures that integrity is not compromised.

5. **Responsiveness**. The governance board should promptly respond to stakeholders who have questions or concerns and to provide honest answers.

6. **Effectiveness and Efficiency**. The governance board must be concerned about the effectiveness and efficiency of their processes with respect to material resources and time.

7. **Equity and Inclusiveness**. Each board member should have an equal seat at the table and should be free to share views and perspectives to enhance and broaden discussions.

8. **Rule of Law**. Good governance means ethical and honest behavior with high integrity; therefore, the governance board must be concerned with

policies and the rule of law. Any of the coaching program's forms for coaching, such as a coaching agreement, should be reviewed by legal counsel.

9. **Strategic Vision**. A board should have a strategic vision to guide and hold board members accountable for their decisions and progress toward their goals. (Price, 2018)

Governance is weak for many new coaching programs in the federal government. We recommend program managers establishing coaching programs educate themselves on governance, enlist others familiar with the function, and consider the nine foundations described by Nicholas Price to build a strong foundation for governance. We also recommend establishing a governance board as soon as possible to ensure the organization's sustainability.

Developing Necessary Policy

We recommend establishing policy as soon as possible. Although what is included in the policy depends on the goals the organization has for coaching, we recommend at a minimum creating a code of ethics and addressing conflicts of interest, confidentiality, and program administration.

Code of Ethics

The policies of an internal coaching program should document a professional code of ethics for coaches of the agency. A professional code of ethics is a formal collection of principles and guidelines of acceptable behavior for the profession. A code establishes a framework for professional behavior and promotes a high standard of practice. Ethics are guides for formulating the thinking of members in a profession when faced with difficult situations with clients. Codes of ethics also serve as a barometer for clients to understand what is considered acceptable behavior by the professional.

Certified internal coaches for federal agencies are expected to adhere to the code of ethics of their credentialing organization. Although OPM does not endorse any specific coach credentialing group, most coach training programs in the United States adhere to guidelines on coaching and ethics published by ICF. Other credentialing organizations include the Center for Credentialing and Education (CCE), European Mentoring and Coaching Council (EMCC), and the Association of Coaching (AC). Federal coaches are expected to abide by ethical standards of conduct defined in the Standards of Ethical Conduct for Employees of the Executive Branch. Also, depending on the mission of the agency, federal coaches may be required to abide by additional ethical behavior standards for their jobs.

Some ethical requirements of a credentialing organization may put specific constraints on the behavior and activities of internal coaches, and these should be considered. For example, coaches possessing the Board-Certified Coach (BCC) credential from CCE may not socialize with clients for two years after the coaching engagement is completed. The CCE deems this unethical behavior. This model was used by CCE because it dovetailed with the ethical standards of therapists but may not be appropriate for internal coaches engaged with employees, who may have a difficult time avoiding colleagues in the workplace.

Conflicts of Interest

All federal employees—including internal coaches—should be well acquainted with the laws for conflict of interest. Policy should address potential conflicts of interest that could arise when coaching employees in their organization. Situations in which internal coaches must consider conflicts of interest include:

- engaging in a coaching relationship with a current direct report
- engaging in a coaching relationship with someone who will imminently become a direct report
- engaging in a coaching relationship with a current manager in their supervisory chain
- engaging in a coaching relationship with federal employees and receiving payment outside of regular salary compensation
- using a coaching relationship as a means of procuring a new job position

Predicting possible future conflicts of interests in any situation can be difficult; however, federal internal coaches should attempt to avoid at the least those situations that present a current conflict of interest.

Limits of Confidentiality

The policy should describe the limits of confidentiality and explain the need for formal coaching agreements when engaging with clients. The policy should also include the need for coaches to inform their clients of the limits of confidentiality by law as it relates to federal employees, including but are not limited to:

- reports of an act of fraud, waste, or abuse
- revelations of having committed a crime
- threats of harm to self or others
- sharing information in violation of a security clearance
- reports of sexual harassment
- requirements by law or a court order to share particular information

The policy should require that the limits on confidentiality are documented in a coaching agreement, which the coach and client are required to sign before coaching begins.

Program Administration

The policy should detail the roles and responsibilities of program administrators, and to a lesser degree of detail, of coaches and clients. The coaching program manager should be designated the main point of contact for the program, including external and internal coaches, coaching clients, leadership, and other organizations. Some program elements to consider:

- determining and communicating how coaching relates to the organizational strategy and mission
- marketing of internal coaching (to include educating the workforce about what coaching is and is not)
- identifying criteria needed both to qualify internal coaches and to continue to engage in coaching others
- the process for requesting a coach
- the process for coach/client matching
- how coaching is tracked
- quality control and evaluation of internal coaching, including both evaluating the coachee outcomes and evaluating the coach's performance level
- remedies for improving quality as needed
- collecting, managing, and reporting coaching metrics required by or useful to the organization, including to whom the data can be made available

Program managers should craft internal processes for developing and supporting the coaching program that complements the needs of their particular organization.

Key Takeaways

- Good governance is critical and foundational for federal coaching programs.
- Program managers should educate themselves and seek assistance from others to establish good governance practices.
- Internal coaching programs must develop governance structures, policies, and practices to support and protect their activities and resources.
- The policy should describe the limits of confidentiality and explain the need for formal coaching agreements when engaging with clients.
- The policies of an internal coaching program should document a professional code of ethics for coaches of the agency.
- The policy should include the need for coaches to inform their clients of the limits of confidentiality by law as it relates to federal employees.
- Policy should address potential conflicts of interest that could arise when working with employees in their organization.
- The policy should detail the roles and responsibilities of program administrators, and to a lesser degree of detail, of coaches and clients.

Key Questions

- What governance structure is necessary for your program?
- What is the best way to develop a policy for your program?
- What other policies exist in your organization that you can use as an example or a template?
- Who in your organization can help you establish a policy?

Reference

Price, N. (2018, August 15). What constitutes good governance? *Diligent*. https://www.diligent.com/insights/corporate-governance/what-constitutes-good-governance/

Supporting Professional Development

8

> The things that we were able to ignite in our partners, our coaches, our mentor coaches, and our facilitators transcended any kind of organizational hierarchy or structure.
>
> Cassandra Brennand

It is commonly recognized that coaching is learned quickly but mastered slowly. However, a certified professional coach can practice coaching as soon as they receive their certification. When a federal government coach starts to coach in their organization, what happens if they run into difficulties? What if there is an ethical concern that the coach has difficulty navigating? What if the client's behavior is unexpected or difficult in some way? Just as governance, discussed in Chapter 7, is important for establishing the credibility of the program in the organization, oversight of the continuous training and development of coaches is important for the success of the coaches in the organization.

Need for Oversight

Many of the helping professions, such as psychology and counseling, require that practitioners be licensed. Licensing boards ensure that unqualified persons do not practice in a profession. They do this by applying a set of standards to determine minimum qualifications. In the United States, the closest thing the coaching profession has to oversight is ICF because it has

DOI: 10.4324/9781003218937-8

published coaching competencies and a code of ethics and has standards for accrediting training and credentialing coaches. ICF is not a licensing board, whose primary purpose would be to protect the public from individuals who may call themselves coaches but will be doing harm to their clients.

What are the federal government's alternatives where oversight is concerned? In 2014, Dr. Wes Long of FDA and A. Myers of HHS offered a credentialing schema for federal coaches which would rival ICF. The proposal included similar levels of credentialing, along with a Certified Federal Mentor Coach, Certified Federal Coach Trainer, Master Certified Federal Coach, and other components. This idea was discussed with the CLOC but not adopted. The CLOC wanted to use a recognized and established credentialing organization, and at the time, many federal agencies required their coaching vendors to hold a credential from ICF.

A Gap in Support

Other helping professionals such as psychologists, counselors, and social workers must also participate in practicums before they are approved to practice unsupervised with clients. Even after psychologists, counselors, and social workers earn their credentials, they are expected to continue to receive mentoring and supervision. In contrast, as of this writing, certified coaches in the United states are required to receive mentoring but are not required to have coaching supervision. This is a gap in the support of coaches in the United States.

FICTP has no requirement to follow up with internal coaches once they complete training. There is no central board in the federal government that oversees coaching standards. FICTP graduates continue to be primarily responsible for their full-time jobs and coach as a collateral duty, which means they may not coach frequently. Over time, they could regress to familiar communication patterns, forgetting coaching techniques and habits learned in training.

At the risk of sounding like alarmists, we believe this creates a danger. Internal coaches risk becoming involved in legal situations, particularly in government workplaces, where there are more stringent or different conflict of interest standards. For example, if a client did something illegal and said, "My coach told me to do it," the situation could create legal problems for everyone involved—the coach, the client (employee), and the organization. Essentially, because the coaching profession is unregulated, client–coach privilege does not exist. Realizing the inherent risks, some federal internal coaches purchase personal liability insurance. This is really the only protection that coaches in the federal government can obtain at this time.

Dr. T. Fitzsimmons was brought back to her agency from an external assignment to manage an education program that would train a large number of internal employees (500) to become certified professional coaches. Initially, the project was all about getting a statement of work together that would attract a contractor who would provide what the agency needed. DIA successfully hired a contractor and made arrangements to train 150 coaches in the first year. After the first cohort kicked off, Dr. T. Fitzsimmons and her co-program manager, C. Covington, began to contemplate the bigger picture for this program. From this early time, Dr. T. Fitzsimmons was concerned about how to bring coaching into the agency in a responsible way. She talked often about "safety."

- **Safety for the Client**. An internal coach who coaches one to three clients at a time is not going to evolve in their expertise as quickly as a coach who is dedicated full time to coaching. The client may be subject to poor coaching.
- **Safety for the Coach**. For the same reasons, the coach may be in danger of collusion or bias. They could make an error and fall easily into mentoring or giving advice. If the coach is violating an ethical boundary, the coach could get into trouble.
- **Safety for the Organization**. As coaches get into trouble, the organization can also be held liable.
- **Safety for the Profession**. If there are increasing numbers of cases of ethical violations and lawsuits against coaches, it could damage the reputation of coaches and the program in general.

Dr. T. Fitzsimmons was concerned that because coaches provided services on a part-time basis, the program's credibility could suffer if coaches forgot their coaching skills and performed in a manner not aligned with ICF coaching principles or if their coaching led to an undesirable or even damaging result. She wondered what the program could do to develop the skills of coaches who would not conduct many hours of coaching and expand their practical coaching experiences. As mentioned earlier in the chapter, if a coach is subpoenaed to testify in a court of law, there is no coach–client privilege. Although Dr. T. Fitzsimmons had no control over whether a coach was subpoenaed, she did have a sense of responsibility to ensure that continuous training opportunities were readily available for the coaches around ethics, core competencies, and other important content.

Dr. T. Fitzsimmons researched what other internal coaching programs were doing to grow coaching capability and discovered few models existed anywhere that DIA could emulate. Most companies with significant investments in coaching hired full-time, credentialed internal coaches. She also found that organizations did provide additional training opportunities. She could not find other organizations who were training large numbers of employees to be part-time coaches.

Coaching Supervision and Coach Mentoring

Many coach training programs expect that coaches will have learned everything necessary to be a coach once they complete their certification program. This expectation is true even for reputable ICF-accredited coach training programs that have a goal to develop coaches qualified at the PCC level. The certification renewal requirements of ICF (and other coaching professional development organizations) require coaches to complete a specific number of hours of continuing education and coach mentoring for some period. Given that coaches work with human beings, is this enough to maintain competency in coaching? We believe that more support for coaches is necessary. This can be achieved through coaching supervision.

> Typically, we take for granted that most of our coaching clients will be "fully functioning individuals" which is less likely in the fields of counseling and therapy. Nonetheless, being the "confidant" on difficult and challenging human issues can be emotionally draining and burdensome at times. Coaching supervision provides the space to share and discuss difficult or challenging clients and to gain support for the emotional impact on you. Conversely, when you have an effective and positive relationship with your client, supervision helps to ensure the work is not just a cozy conversation and enables you to challenge them effectively too... Coaching supervision provides the opportunity to stand back, with the setting of a confidential relationship, to help you reflect and better understand what supports or damages the client work you do.
>
> (Clutterbuck et al., 2016)

In the United States, although supervision to support psychologists has existed for several decades, supervision for coaches is only just becoming known as a helpful practice. ICF does support coaches who have supervision by allowing continuing education credit when applying for coach credential renewal. In contrast, coaches in the United Kingdom must provide evidence of receiving coaching supervision in their coaching contracts. In the United States, few new coach training programs incorporate coaching supervision in their programs. Nor do they educate new coaches that supervision is a necessary practice for their continuing development as a coach.

On the other hand, coach mentoring is definitely supported by ICF. Coaches at the ICF ACC level are required to have 10 hours of coach mentoring as a part of their credentialing process and for their credential renewal every three years.

Although less than a handful of programs offer coaching supervision in the United States, coach training programs that do include coaching supervision help coaches learn to depend on coaching supervision when they run into an ethical dilemma or struggle with a client. The global coaching profession is clear that coaches need the support of coaching supervisors. The ICF website provides definitions of coaching supervision and coach mentoring. The problem in the federal government is that internal coaches have limited opportunities to work with coach mentors, and even fewer opportunities to work with coaching supervisors.

- **ICF Definition of Coaching Supervision.** "Focuses on development of the coach's capacity through offering a richer and broader opportunity for support and development." (International Coaching Federation, n.d.)
- **ICF Definition of Coach Mentoring.** "For an ICF credential consists of coaching and feedback in a collaborative, appreciative, and dialogued process based on an observed or recorded coaching session to increase the coach's capability in coaching, in alignment with ICF Core Competencies." (International Coaching Federation, n.d.)

Dr. T. Fitzsimmons and A. Myers are trained coaching supervisors and ICF-registered mentors. They understand the need and value of both coach mentoring and coaching supervision. Until ICF certifications include a requirement for coaching supervision, the coaching community in the United States—including the federal government coaching community—will struggle to incorporate this important support function into their programs. We hope that supervision will eventually become required for all credentialed coaches. More federal coaches are getting trained in the coaching supervision process. More will be needed in the future to support the growing number of internal coaches in the federal government.

Coaching programs in the federal government interested in coaching supervision can purchase these services from trained professionals. A list of coaching supervisors can be found on the website for the Association for Coaching Supervisors (https://www.associationofcoachingsupervisors.com). A list of registered coach mentors can be found on the ICF website (https://coachingfedaration.com).

In lieu of training or procuring professional coaching supervisors, coaching programs in the federal government could encourage coaches to serve as peer supervisors for both individuals and groups. There are several supervision models and processes that could be used. Of course, it would be better if peer supervisors had the appropriate training and oversight conducted by a trained professional coaching supervisor.

Socializing coaching supervision at DIA has not been easy. The word "supervision" was very problematic because many employees assumed it meant the person who was the "boss." Dr. T. Fitzsimmons continued to inform coaches about the need for supervision by conducting webinars to demonstrate supervision techniques. She interviewed coaching supervision experts Dr. Peter Hawkins and Sam Magill and conducted follow-on discussions with coaches. She also conducted community of practice events where she introduced coaching supervision and demonstrated it to the participants in one-on-one and fishbowl demonstrations.

Dr. T. Fitzsimmons continued to be challenged to identify the best course of action to make coaching supervision common place. Both individual and group supervision was offered at DIA but it was limited to the capacity and time available of Dr. T. Fitzsimmons and C. Covington. Dr. T. Fitzsimmons and her colleague promoted the idea of more advanced coaches becoming coach supervisors. One idea they considered was to develop in-house training to teach peer supervision. They also considered policy that would require supervision for all coaches at DIA. This approach would create greater need for supervision and enable a stronger case for funding (Browning et al., 2022).

Dr. T. Fitzsimmons also trained mentor coaches by delivering instruction that delved deeply into ICF competencies, had them coach each other, and assess recordings of coaching sessions. This training accelerated the coaches' learning and took them to a whole new level of competence in coaching. Coach mentoring instruction reenergized their enthusiasm for coaching; they immediately applied their learning to client relationships. All of the community of practice learning events have had a similar impact.

Why Coaches Need Continuous Professional Development

There are many things that can be done for continuing professional development of coaches, and coaching program managers are only limited by their imagination and funding. Let's review why it is important to have continuous development for coaches.

- It is a best practice for coaches who wish to become members of professional bodies and must demonstrate commitment to continuing development. For example, ICF requires 40 hours of CEU for renewal of a credential every three years.
- It is a way of ensuring that coaches continuously improve and that the quality of their coaching remains high.
- It allows coaches to expand their skills.
- Delivering professional development or training as a group with your coaches present helps build your community of practice.

Federal Coaching Professional Development and Community Support

In our interviews, we found evidence that federal coaching programs provided organized continuing education, community of practice events, and coach mentoring. Other programs shared their need for a community of practice and training for their coaches. In this section, we describe the approaches from four programs.

Housing and Urban Development Coaching Conference

In 2016, individual agencies were creating their own internal coaching programs to provide coaching to their own agency personnel. In June 2016, the first Housing and Urban Development (HUD) Federal Coaching Conference was held. It was sponsored by FICTP graduate and Chief Human Capital Officer Towanda Brooks and Chief Learning Officer Dr. Sheila Wright (Dr. S. Wright) and was open to coaches across the federal government. Dr. S. Wright addressed the conference participants:

In an effort to build a better HUD, the focus of this learning event is to promote, educate, and embed a coaching culture throughout the agency and federal government at large. It is our belief that by implementing effective coaching strategies, we can enhance leadership ability, improve performance, and increase employee engagement.

Dr. S. Wright also recognized the community:

Special thanks to our partners who are sharing their coaching knowledge and experience. We truly appreciate your support, leadership, and ability to see the vision of a federal coaching culture. During this conference, we ask participants to stay engaged and proactive as we shape the future of coaching.

In 2018, HUD held another conference based on the first conference's huge success. The organizers enlisted presenters from federal organizations and even paid for a few speakers. Magda Mook, Chief Executive Officer of ICF, was keynote speaker. They opened the conference to other federal organizations and 350 participants attended, and it proved to be an effective strategy for the HUD Coaching Program to gain more access to the broader network of federal coaches. They managed to deliver a robust agenda of learning events that met the needs of new and experienced coaches. It was a service to the entire federal coaching community and brought attention to its own internal coaching program and to HUD employees and leadership. It was a win–win event all the way around!

Federal Coaching Network

FCN is a simple yet large network of coaches from across the government, many of whom have graduated from FICTP. In 2022, the FCN database contained over 1,500 names and is the platform the community uses to promote opportunities and events.

In 2022, FCN was managed by Elizabeth (Liz) Winters, Coaching Program Manager at OPM. The FCN Listserv (federalcoachingnetwork@opm. gov) communicates coaching opportunities, open positions, and upcoming learning events. FCN also sponsors a quarterly webinar for all coaches that is well attended. These quarterly webinars are one of two government-wide activities that bring federal coaches together as a community.

Government Coaching Community of Practice

Since 2011, Larry Westberg of DoD has led the ICF DC Metro sponsored community of practice with a distribution list of almost 1,000 names. He offers a monthly one-hour event on different topics that award ICF-approved CEUs. The Government Coaching Community of Practice is open to anyone in government, including contractors.

Evolving Continuing Education Curriculum

One program learned that continuing education curricula must evolve as coaches become more experienced. They developed a curriculum that could be implemented in stages. In 2015, the program consisted of 80 coaches and only eight were credentialed. Program managers focused on coaching awareness/ networking events, coaching skills in the workplace sessions, and coaching certification classes, with some continuing education and mentoring for several years. In 2021, the program had over 200 coaches, 90 credentialed (several were ICF-accredited PCCs), and they had added more continuing education sessions, master coaching events, annual mentor coaching sessions, and were exploring coach supervision. Their website offers a virtual community of practice for resources, asynchronous training, and discussion boards available only to coaches.

DIA Coaching Program Community of Practice

In considering what the coaching program at DIA could do to provide ongoing growth opportunities for coaches, Dr. T. Fitzsimmons launched a community of practice for the coaches to interact regularly and share ideas, challenges, and perspectives. The community of practice training sessions, seminars, and webinars were centered around a skill-building webinar taught by her, her co-manager, or someone in the community.

Dr. T. Fitzsimmons knew policy played an important role in the success of the coaching program at DIA and worked to publish internal policy that described the role of coaches, how coaching is conducted, and credentialing requirements, including a requirement that coaches conduct 24 hours of coaching and attend a minimum of three community of practice events annually. She obtained approval to conduct in-house coach education that qualified for ICF-approved CEUs and supported coaches-in-training to progress toward ICF certification. In 2021, the program delivered continuing

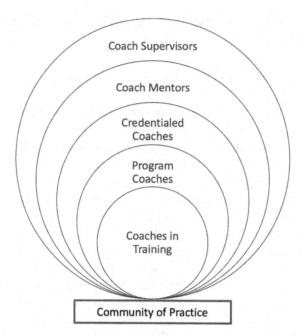

Figure 8.1 Coaching Ecosystem at DIA

coach education on ethics in coaching, advanced core competencies, and other special topics that qualified for over 120 CEUs. The program's curriculum included presentations from industry experts as the budget permitted.

Over time, an ecosystem organically emerged generating opportunities for continued growth and learning for coaches that was further strengthened by creating mentor coaches. Figure 8.1 details the different coaching roles of this ecosystem.

The ecosystem depicted in Figure 8.1 is dependent on the continuous influx of new coaches who are training to become certified coaches. As these coaches complete their certification requirements, they become "program coaches" and provide professional coaching to DIA employees. They also assume the role of coach to other coaches in training, who get to experience being coached by someone who recently completed the same training program. Program coaches interested in further developing their skills take additional training to become coach mentors and support both program coaches and coaches in training. Some program coaches will choose to obtain an ICF credential and join the ranks of credentialed coaches. Finally, those interested in further professional development may become a registered coach mentor, and a smaller percentage may pursue coaching supervision. All members of the ecosystem share in learning during community of practice events.

Other Recommendations for Continuous Professional Development

The following ideas are inspired by Katherine St John-Brooks (2013) in her book *Internal Coaching—The Inside Story*.

Skills Practices. The goal is to offer coaches the opportunity to practice in a safe environment and to get feedback from their client and at least one observer. This can easily be done in coaching triads where each person takes a turn in the role of coach, client, and observer. A variation is to have a group of coaches meet and observe a coach–client pair coach for the whole group. The group of participants includes at least one "expert" observer who gives targeted feedback. It is important to ask the observers to give only one point of positive feedback and that only the expert observer gives constructive criticism. This approach is based on positive psychology and creates safety for all the participants. If you record the session, you can provide more detailed feedback to the coach at a later time. Dr. T. Fitzsimmons experienced triads and skill practices in a variety of programs in which she was a student and an instructor. She observed that no matter what the role, each participant stood to gain significant learning about the coaching process.

Special Topics. You can offer the coaches something new, like a new model or concept they have not learned before. Examples include:

- somatic coaching
- neurolinguistic programming
- neuroscience
- systemic approach
- narrative coaching
- using metaphor or any other coaching skill
- life purpose
- team coaching
- group coaching
- peer coaching

Books. Authors are often happy to talk about their books. Dr. Fitzsimmons recalls when Marcia Reynolds provided an introduction to *Coach the Person, Not the Problem* (2020) to DIA coaches during the 2021 International Coaching Week. The session was delivered via webinar and hard-copy and electronic versions of the book were made available to the coaches.

Whole Day Events or Conferences. If you are on a low budget, or even if budget is not an issue, you can ask your coaches to participate in planning and delivering the event. For example, at the 2021 International Coaching

Week, a combination of sessions were designed, developed, and delivered by coaches, each with an area of expertise. Here are some of the agenda items on DIA's virtual International Coaching Week agenda.

- **What is Coaching?** Offered to the entire workforce.
- **Pop-up Coaching.** Conducted in a virtual space in breakout rooms. The idea came from the coaches who also ran the program.
- **Write to Thrive! Exploring the Power of Creative Reflective Writing to Flourish in Turbulent Times**. A paid event conducted by Drs. Karyn Prentice and Elaine Patterson.
- **Experiencing the "As-If" Mind Meditation.** For coaches, designed and conducted by Dr. Virginia Sargent.
- **Vertical Development/Adult Development: A Coaching Framework.** A paid event conducted by Dr. Chris Wahl.
- **Peer Coaching: An introduction for all audiences**. Designed and conducted by Dr. T. Fitzsimmons.
- **Team Coaching.** An introduction to team coaching for all audiences. This was a live demonstration conducted by Dr. T. Fitzsimmons.

Online Resources. There are many books and resources available about coaching. An organization can decide what it should buy and gain access to continuous professional development for the coaches. One option is to record webinars that are internally delivered and archive them in a location where coaches can gain access to them. Dr. T. Fitzsimmons used ICF's rule for allowing a coach to view a webinar online and make an appointment with the instructor to review the learning. The conversation is a rich one-on-one learning opportunity for the coach and an opportunity for Dr. Fitzsimmons to know the coach better. The coach is then allowed to claim full credit for the webinar as if they had attended, plus the time spent talking with Dr. T. Fitzsimmons. Otherwise, the videos may be viewed and claimed as resource development credits in the ICF credit system.

Title: Coaching Chat and Chew at the DOD

Coaching Chat and Chew at the DOD

For some, there could be many reasons to not get involved in taking on challenging tasks with no apparent reward and incentive. This was not the story Nichole Meade of the Defense Information Systems Agency told herself.

A graduate of the FICTP, she saw the need to create a community of practice where coaches in the federal government could come together and share information and be supported along their coaching journeys in the government space. N. Meade created that supportive environment with a monthly lunchtime event called "Coaching Chat and Chew." She knew there were many coaches throughout the federal government who could share information and wanted an opportunity for all coaches to learn about and from each other and begin building a network.

N. Meade had the vision and the tenacity to find out what she needed to do to make this happen. Who should she invite? How would she get content? What technology would be best for delivery? She personally pursued the answers to these questions and moved forward with the monthly event using MS Teams, and the Department of Defense Coaching Community and beyond are better for it.

The objective of the Chat and Chew is to be the place where coaches and non-coaches alike can learn more about coaching, coaching skills, and planting the seeds for a coaching culture in the federal government. The agenda includes a live coaching session each month with a federal coach and volunteer client. These sessions show what coaching is and what it is not. It also provides a forum to watch other coaches in action to get different perspectives, questions, tools, and techniques. The target audience was initially for coaches, but N. Meade realized for coaching to be successful everyone needs to learn about coaching. The target audience now is the target audience for federal coaching—all military and civilian employees. Approximately 60 people join each month from across the federal government, coaches, and non-coaches alike. More and more people ask to be included in the distribution list, which indicates there is value in attending. These discussions are very valuable and always provide a nugget of wisdom that all participants can take away. A few of the topics presented include:

- Coaching culture
- Credentialing
- Team/group coaching
- Assessments
- Coaching skills for leaders/managers
- Coaching presence
- Asking powerful questions
- The coach–client relationship

N. Meade reflected on what she learned since the rollout of the Chat and Chew. She learned that it works to try different ideas out and to see how they resonate with the audience. Her hope is that other supervisors/leaders/managers are as supportive as her own have been and allow their staff to try things out. She also discovered that through coaching and other workforce development programs we enjoy a different avenue for feedback from the workforce to understand what is happening.

Key Takeaways

- Planning for the future was key to developing the initial training programs.
- For coaching, the most important reason for continuing to invest in the coaches' growth is to ensure safety for the client, the coach, the agency, and the profession. Another important reason is to help coaches develop their capacity to coach.
- In a federal coaching program in which the cadre is part-time, providing more growth opportunities is important, given the lesser amount of coaching that they will have an opportunity to do. You are really racing against time and a human being's ability to forget what they learn if it is not frequently reinforced with experience.
- Coaching supervision focuses on development of the coach's capacity through offering a richer and broader opportunity for support and development.
- Coach mentoring consists of coaching and feedback in a collaborative, appreciative dialogue process based on an observed or recorded coaching session to increase the coach's capability in coaching, in alignment with the ICF Core Competencies.
- The coaching program's continuous learning support systems should include a number of elements. Whatever opportunities for training that exist would certainly be appreciated by the coaches.
- As the coaching program grows, more experienced coaches can be set up to support newer coaches through mentoring. Mentoring and supervision should be provided to the coaches. If not provided, they should be required to be obtained.

Key Questions

- How will you determine the coach training needs for your program?

- What kind of ongoing support is needed for your program and how would will you plan for it?
- How will you evolve training as your cadre matures?

References

Browning, J., Fitzsimmons, T., & Arnold J. (2022). Internal coaching supervision: Insights into two US based cases and perspectives. In *Coaching supervision: Voices from the Americas* (1st ed., pp. 149–167). Routledge.

Clutterbuck, D., Whitaker, C., & Lucas, M. (2016). *Coaching supervision: A practical guide for supervisees*. Routledge.

International Coaching Federation. (n.d.). Coaching supervision. Retrieved January 1, 2022, from https://coachingfederation.org/coaching-supervision

International Coaching Federation. (n.d.). Mentor coaching. Retrieved January 1, 2022, from https://coachingfederation.org/mentor-coaching

Reynolds, M. (2020). *Coach the person, not the problem: A guide to using reflective inquiry*. Barrett-Koehler Publishers.

St. John-Brooks, K. (2013). *Internal coaching: The inside story*. Routledge.

Contemplating the Future 9

With the seeds that we've laid, I think it's going to just keep growing...I see the future blossoming.

Randy Bergquist

When we contemplate the future of coaching in the federal government, we imagine what the workplace would be like if coaching became so mainstream that it was integrated into many aspects of human and social development, like training, leadership, recruiting, and hiring. In this chapter, we make predictions about what will happen in the coaching arena, especially in government organizations, and we identify emerging professional trends worth monitoring.

Coaching Stays and Grows

Ultimately, what does success look like for coaching in the federal government? Will every employee have a coach? Will we have a coaching culture across government—one that questions, listens, dreams, and considers options rather than depending on the status quo? We believe both will be true, and to an extent are already true today. Coaching in the federal government is here to stay, and at the very least, employees can seek out a coach to work on their personal and professional goals.

In 2021, a study published by the Human Capital Institute indicated that between 2019 and 2020, coaching and mentoring decreased from 12 to 14 on the list of human resource strategic priorities. At the same time, organizations

DOI: 10.4324/9781003218937-9

were prioritizing people-oriented strategies: retention of high-performers remained the highest priority and effective teams made a steep climb in 2020, compared to 2019. Likewise, the priority status of employee engagement and experience, workforce planning, change management, and diversity and inclusion increased in 2020 (Filipkowski, 2021).

The most dramatic increase in prioritization was DEI strategies. We believe that coaching will become the enabler for these human-centered priorities.

We agree with pioneer C. Allen that the belief "everyone (in government) is a leader, and everyone gets a coach" will drive continued growth in coaching for the federal government. Employees will expect coaching to be included in their workplace benefits packages. According to Fred Kofman, Google Leadership Coach and author of *The Meaning Revolution*, job seekers are less interested in material incentives and more interested in non-material benefits that create inspiring workplaces and personal growth opportunities—like coaching (Mejia, 2018).

Recent college graduates are already familiar with the benefits of coaching because colleges and career placement organizations rely on it. We predict that coaching will become a normal part of employee benefits and healthcare options in the federal government. Many of our interviewees agreed with this prediction of expansion.

Coach-Like Approaches Become an Expectation

As coaching becomes more popular and prevalent, the workforce will expect supervisors and others to use coaching skills as a first approach in workplace conversations, including orienting new employees to their work responsibilities, exploring individual development plans, and performance appraisal conversations. In fact, leaders may find themselves using coach-like skills in hallway and elevator conversations. It will become a common approach in leadership communications. Leaders who are basically unapproachable or lack the ability to listen to employees, ask questions, and allow for individual contributions will lose their influence in the workplace.

Coaching Skills Training Becomes Prominent

As a result of the rising expectation that leaders possess coach-like skills, we believe the training of coach-like skills in the workplace will spread. This will involve teaching both managers and employees how to listen, question, reframe, and empower others to create their own action and accountability plans. According to R. Hansen, "the biggest ROI may not be in creating professional coaches but in leveraging coaching skills for leaders and team members." Coaching skills can unleash the potential of employees and leaders and increase respectful engagement. Thus, increased coaching skills training to support daily operations across the federal government will result in increased ROI.

The Profession Becomes More Defined

Credentialing standards for coaching will continue to become more defined as the number of certified coaches increases. In the 2000s, it was acceptable for a coach to simply have a certificate from a coaching school to be a professional coach. By 2021, organizations had learned to ask for specific credentialing such as, ACC, PCC, and Master Certified Coaches (MCC) offered by ICF for important coaching projects. Also, ICF requirements are becoming more rigorous. In 2022, the testing requirements for the Coach Knowledge Assessment (CKA) became more stringent, requiring proctoring in a testing center or at home with special arrangements for live proctoring.

At the time of this writing, many agencies had guidelines requiring coaches to be trained and certified by a credentialing body. We believe the federal government will continue to create policies that match or exceed the changes to standards occurring in the coaching community. We also believe OPM will eventually create a job series and standards for coaching.

For years, the coaching profession worked to differentiate itself from other helping services, such as mentoring, counseling, and psychotherapy. We believe confusion and competition between coaching and the other helping services will continue. The coaching profession must continue to educate the public about coaching's role, value, and ROI. As healthcare professionals and therapists explicitly leverage a coach-like approach in their practices, competition between coaching and these helping services will intensify. Coaching may follow the footsteps of *counselors*, a term freely used by people offering helping services but who had various and inconsistent levels of preparation qualifying them to do so. In the 1980s, lawmakers passed legislation regulating counseling to protect the public from people who might do harm and requiring that counselors be credentialed or licensed. If coaching was similarly regulated, only licensed or credentialed coaches could identify themselves as a *coach*. We do not know if this will happen for the coaching profession, but we support increased regulation, given that it would have the same effect—to remove those coaches who might do harm (Carnahan & Jungers, 2015).[1]

Coach Training Becomes More Accessible

Coach development, support, and credentialing will continue to evolve. In 2021, ICF approved training program owners to increase the amount of asynchronously delivered content in their programs. This opening up of standards will increase availability of both initial and recurrent training for coaches, which will become more commonplace and accessible and hopefully will decrease training costs, an especially helpful change for coaching programs in the federal government, working with tight budgets.

Mentoring and Coaching Supervision Become Commonplace

Increased mentor coaching and coaching supervision will result in the development of more credible coaches and will immediately and positively affect the quality and growth of established coaching programs. In the United States, mentor coaching is common and included in many federal coach training programs (including FICTP). Unfortunately, most internal coaches are unfamiliar with coaching supervision. The U.S. coaching community must commit both time and resources to embrace coaching supervision as has occurred in the European coaching community. According to Jackie Arnold (2014):

> Supervision is essential for all coaches and may be more critical at specific times than others. As a guideline, supervision should occur after 15–20 sessions of coaching, but support and guidance may be needed more regularly, particularly in pressured environments.

Coaching supervision keeps coaches engaged and invested in their development and we believe it will expand in federal organizations.

Artificial Intelligence Becomes Part of the Coaching Picture

We believe technology—specifically artificial intelligence (AI)—will change the landscape in which coaching is delivered, become part of every coaching program's strategy, and support the mass proliferation of coaching in all its formats. Chatbots are routinely used in marketing and customer service. Triggered by key words or questions, users see tailored responses that specifically address their needs. Chatbots are commonly used in interactions at banks, pizza deliveries, and online retailers.

Although human coaches will always be part of the coaching landscape, clients can conduct a lot of self-reflection using AI applications. They can also use AI applications to support on-demand interactions for routine situations ("How can you find a mentor?") with junior employees or for check-ins ("What are you learning during your performance reviews?") when coaches are unavailable for senior staff.

With new companies delivering large-scale coaching to organizations, many see the potential of providing coaching and instruction together as part of the employee development process. Technology platforms with AI will be available and make it easier for employees to quickly either access a coach or use an app for quick support.

Team and Group Coaching Become Prominent

The momentum created by both team and group coaching will continue to grow. Much of this growth will be due to better use of resources and the preference of individuals who appreciate group interaction as a means of learning. As discussed in Chapter 6, there is clearly a role for team and group coaching in the federal government. As more coaches become trained to work with teams and groups, these services will flourish because they allow coaches to reach more clients and allow clients to share and grow with each other.

Coaching Niches Take Root

Although pioneers described failed attempts to combine coaching with conflict coaching and career coaching, we believe that these two and other coaching niches (e.g., retirement coaching, financial coaching, nutrition coaching, weight loss coaching) will increase.

In 2020, early in the COVID-19 pandemic, the popularity of coaching increased as many employees focused on life changes and worked to develop greater self-awareness. The pandemic changed the way many people think about the workplace and blurred the separation between home and work. Employees had to *bring* their entire selves to their workplaces, as many worked from home, and this thinking continues as they redefine the value of work. Coaching supports all aspects of employees' lives, both personal and professional. Coaches focused on supporting niches will provide that best support.

Title: NIWC Pacific: Department of the Navy

Bringing Passion to Work Makes a Difference

Angela Falcini describes running a coaching program as "the joy of my career." A. Falcini is a project manager and a Scientist at NIWC Pacific, under the Naval Information Warfare Systems Command. She was personally interested in Coaching and pursued a certification with iPEC in 2016. She was not aware of the Federal Coach Network, the FICTP, or anything related to coaching in the federal government. She originally thought she would use her coaching skills as a side business because it was her passion. She never imagined that her organization would take it on as a developmental opportunity for staff. How wrong she was! Toward the end of her coaching program, she met with her division director to share information about her experience and the coaching process. She shared her vision of offering coaching services to everyone in the organization, not just the senior executives, managers, and supervisors who were coached through DAU, or through a contract. She explained that coaching would be particularly helpful for technical employees and scientists in developing leadership behaviors. This meeting had been scheduled for 30 minutes, but her division director was so intrigued that the meeting went for 2.5 hours. A. Falcini recommended creating a pilot coaching program for engineers and scientists who had been individual contributors and were recently placed in leadership roles. The division director approved the approach and secured a small amount of funding to support it. They started the process of identifying who might be good clients. The effort at first was small, with A. Falcini and a handful of other certified coaches from sister organizations across the Navy providing the coaching. Glowing testimonials were collected from the clients on their career progression and promotions. Over two fiscal years, 27 out of 40 coaching clients received promotions after they began the coaching process. A. Falcini was able to secure more funding to train 18 more internal coaches.

Much of A. Falcini's success had to do with her ability to gather data and make compelling cases to senior leaders. She recruited her own Senior Leader Champion with one of these cases to help grow the program beyond the initial NIWC Pacific organization of 5,000+ civilians to the NAVWAR Command of 11,000+. While she started the coaching program in 2017, A. Falcini asked for a more conservative approach before expanding further to the entire Command. She was a Program Manager in an Operational side of the business and didn't want the "horse to start galloping and [she] lose control of the reins." So, leveraging other resources and going slow and learning the process was the best course of action. An ongoing challenge for A. Falcini is managing the polarity of using working capital funds versus mission-related appropriated funds for this work. Her vision of the future involves creating a coaching culture across her entire organization and beyond. To achieve this, she would first need to become a full-time program manager for coaching. She would grow the coaching cadre to 3 percent of the organization's population. In addition, she would introduce coaching-skills training to leaders and teach peer coaching to others. She also talked about creating "mastermind groups" across the organization to support leaders and individual contributors. The future also entails working with the larger DoD's vision for coaching and partnering with other DoD coaches to gain support, provide coaching, and share best practices. A. Falcini reiterated her three biggest challenges were, "Funding, Funding, and Funding." Even with funding, she sees a need for a more solid ROI model at the federal level. This would help in telling the story of coaching and its benefits to the organization and the federal government. With the support from other DoD and Federal coaches in the community, the future looks bright.

Key Takeaways

- Coaching activities and a coaching culture will continue to benefit and grow within the federal sector.
- Coaching is not going away. It's too good of an idea for communications in the workplace to become more coach-like for leaders and others.
- As the profession becomes more prominent, the requirements will become more defined by the professional organizations as well as the federal government.
- Coach Supervision as well as Coach Mentoring will become a requirement for credentialing as well as for the practice of coaching in organizations.
- Team Coaching will become a very important part of coaching in the organization.
- Artificial intelligence applications will soon be a part of coach offerings offered by external companies.
- Constantly evolving contexts within your organization will affect the coaching program.
- Adaptation can promote health with any organization.

Key Questions

- How will the constantly evolving contexts within your organization affect your coaching program?
- How can you prepare yourself and your organization to meet the evolving coaching needs for the next two years? The next ten years?

References

Arnold, J. (2014). *Coaching supervision at its BEST*. Crown House Publishing.

Carnahan, B., & Jungers, C. (2015, November 10). Understanding how counselors are regulated. *Counseling Today: A publication of the American Counseling Association*. https://ct.counseling.org/2015/11/understanding-how-counselors-are-regulated/

Filipkowski, J. (2021, January 14). *2021 talent pulse priorities*. Human Capital Institute. https://www.hci.org/research/2021-talent-pulse-priorities

Mejia, Z. (2018, May 18). Google leadership coach: The best way to attract high-performing employees doesn't cost a dime. *CNBC.com*. https://www.cnbc.com/2018/05/02/google-coach-the-best-way-to-attract-high-performing-employees-is-free.html

Note

1 See the American Counseling Association website, Licensure Requirements for Professional Counselors A State by State Report (https://www.counseling.org/knowledge-center/licensure-requirements) for more information about the development of the counseling profession in the United States.

An Opportunity for Change   **10**

> Coaching has created a new way of having conversations and creating a coaching culture through those conversations. We are helping to really transform how people are supported in the government. It helps people to be their best, and if we're helping others to be their best, we get to be our best too.
>
> Lynn Feingold

We began this journey exploring two simple questions:

- What can we learn about coaching in the federal government, from our personal experiences and the experiences of nearly 40 colleagues, that we can share with others?
- What useful insights about organizational change can we glean from the coaching movement in the federal government?

We have done our best to document and share what we have learned about the nuances of building and maintaining a successful coaching program in the federal government. Perhaps others cultivating a coaching program in private industry will also find the information in this book useful.

We did not intend for this book to be about implementing large organizational change; countless books already exist on this topic. We wanted to study and think about the change created through coaching. The federal government now has a group of employees trained to coach others. They do it for a range of reasons, including to provide service to the public beyond

DOI: 10.4324/9781003218937-10

their regular jobs, to continue their personal growth and learning, and to gain coaching hours for credentialing purposes.

Now, with a cadre of trained coaches, we realize the federal government has an opportunity to use coaching as a tool for change, where change is truly needed.

Two Areas Where Coaching Can Help

At the time of this writing, there are seemingly unsolvable problems facing the United States and the world. A global pandemic has persisted for two years, climate change is creating catastrophic weather events, and viewpoints are deeply polarized on these and other societal issues. These challenges impact, and are impacted by, all levels of government. In Chapter 1, we asked readers to imagine the federal government with a culture that values and uses coaching skills and where senior leaders, managers, and employees:

- explore expectations, needs, opportunities, and challenges with an open mind
- listen actively and ask questions
- identify options and consider barriers
- design plans with accountability
- approach daily work with a growth mindset

We believe greater potential exists for government to impact troubling issues if a broader and deeper culture of coaching is cultivated, supported by certified coaches, and by managers and leaders trained in coach-like skills. Two areas we believe coaching can help:

- advance workplace diversity, equity, inclusion, accessibility (DEIA) and belonging
- address general dissatisfaction with leaders in the government workplace

Diversity, Equity, Inclusion, Accessibility, and Belonging

In June 2021, President Biden signed an Executive Order on Diversity, Equity, Inclusion, and Accessibility in the federal workforce. This action requires government agencies to focus on increasing DEIA in the workplace.

As the Nation's largest employer, the Federal Government must be a model for diversity, equity, inclusion, and accessibility, where all employees are treated with dignity and respect. Accordingly, the Federal Government must strengthen its ability to recruit, hire, develop, promote, and retain our Nation's talent and remove barriers to equal opportunity. It must also provide resources and opportunities to strengthen and advance diversity, equity, inclusion, and accessibility across the Federal Government. The Federal Government should have a workforce that reflects the diversity of the American people. A growing body of evidence demonstrates that diverse, equitable, inclusive, and accessible workplaces yield higher-performing organizations.

(Exec. Order No. 14,035, 2021)

As the quote suggests, ensuring equal opportunity in government is a worthy challenge for more than just becoming a fair reflection of the diversity of the American people.

Research indicates that the best chance for addressing challenging problems is bringing together people with different backgrounds and experiences. Diversity brings strength. McKinsey & Company examined 180 companies across four countries over two years and found that diverse boards perform better than their less diverse counterparts (Barta et al., 2012).

Unfortunately, decision makers in the federal government are not a diverse group. In a 2021 study conducted by Partnership for Public Service:

As of March 2021, people of color represent 47% of all full-time, entry-level employees but only 33% of senior-level positions. And within the Senior Executive Service—the elite corps of experienced civil servants responsible for leading the federal workforce—the disparity is even wider. Only 23% of all career SES members are people of color.

(Lardy, 2021)

The noticeable lack of diversity in the higher grades of the federal government creates a potential problem of bias, both conscious and unconscious. "Unconscious (or implicit) bias is a term that describes the associations we hold, outside our conscious awareness and control. Unconscious bias can have a significant influence on our attitudes and behaviors, especially towards other people." (Imperial College London, n.d.). Bias and unconscious bias can be at play when decisions are made with respect to hiring and promotions.

In addition, when homogeneous groups agree on a variety of issues (perhaps they share a bias consciously or unconsciously) without any dissension, they may be experiencing a phenomenon known as *groupthink*. Here are examples of homogeneous groups—although the list could be endless:

- any group of any particular race
- any group of any particular religion
- any group of immigrants from any country
- any group from a particular region or state
- any group from any particular political party or organization

According to Jennifer Garvey Berger (2019), there is a biological reason for groupthink. In order to survive, human beings are conditioned to agree with each other. She calls it a "mind trap." This mind trap or bias is the barrier we want to break so that we can enjoy the benefits of diversity and we can get to a government workplace that enjoys equity, inclusion, and belonging. To leverage diversity and to make it our nation's strength rather than a workplace problem we are trying to solve, we must address these biologically based behaviors intentionally.

While this book does not cover the topics of DEIA or belonging and unconscious bias in great depth and there is no one solution for these complex challenges, we believe coaching has the potential to make a big difference in changing thinking and behaviors in the federal government. Those who learn to coach, and others who learn coach-like skills, learn how to actively listen to their fellow human beings with curiosity and empathy.

The government employees with the greatest potential to have the greatest impact on DEIA—especially belonging—are leaders (team leaders, supervisors, managers, senior executives). Leaders who become certified coaches have learned to ask powerful questions and hear the views, struggles, dreams, and goals of others. They have increased ability to express empathy and appreciation. Over time, they will appreciate their employees to a greater degree than they did prior to coach training.

In a typical ICF-approved coach training program, participants learn that to be effective, they must be self-aware and understand their own biases. They achieve clarity by learning to surrender to their own vulnerabilities with humility, curiosity, and self-compassion. Whatever their ethnicity, race, sexual orientation, abilities, challenges, or experiences, these coaches learn to identify and understand what their biases mean as they coach someone different than themselves. They learn how to act with self-compassion when their "inner critics" show up. This ability uniquely equips them to work with others and reframe situations, if or when the thinking of individuals or groups becomes stuck.

Although it would be great if this was enough, it is naïve to think that coach training is all we need to address this complex challenge. In our interview with Mavis Johnson (M. Johnson), a coach in the federal government with 18 years of experience, we realized that a typical coach training program may not be enough to prepare leaders and coaches to truly be effective in addressing the issues of DEIA. M. Johnson attended a coaching program whose foundation was about DEIA. The participants were directly immersed in discussions about significant issues for marginalized groups, intersectionality, and other things integral to diversity, equity, inclusion, and accessibility. "They pushed us to have really candid conversations and to examine our own relationship with and to power," she said. Training programs for coaches and others who learn coach-like skills need to have a focus on DEIA, along with power dynamics and emotional intelligence, to better address these complex issues. If coach training programs had a strong foundation in DEIA, it would be even more likely that the unconscious biases of participants would be revealed, and that they would be more equipped to have discussions in the workplace that make a difference.

Dissatisfaction with Leaders

OPM conducts FEVS annually. Historically, some questions that assess communication, empowerment, performance, and senior leadership receive the lowest level of agreement from respondents. Table 10.1, adapted from U.S. Office of Personnel Management (2020), presents employee response rates to ten FEVS questions about management and leaders in 2020. FEVS results indicated that generally, employees in the federal government do not trust that their leaders have their best interests at heart. Clearly, further study is necessary to interpret the data and understand why employees responded as they did. We assume the FEVS results are due at least in part to lack of communication between leaders and the workforce at every level.

Based on the limited ROI results discussed in Chapter 2, applying coach-like skills throughout all levels of management—team leaders, supervisors, managers, and senior executives—is one tangible step that agencies could take to impact the low ratings reported to OPM in FEVS 2020. As M. Johnson shared, "The coaching model helps people have different types of conversations, it opens the door to a different type of inquiry." When leaders and their subordinates are trained how to use coach-like skills, they learn to:

Table 10.1 2020 Lowest Percentage Level of Agreement Responses

Total Employee Response	FEVS Question
42%	In my work unit, steps are taken to deal with a poor performer who cannot or will not improve. (Q. 10)
43%	I believe the results of this survey will be used to make my agency a better place to work. (Q. 18)
51%	In my work unit, differences in performance are recognized in a meaningful way. (Q. 12)
51%	In my organization, senior leaders generate high levels of motivation and commitment in the workforce. (Q. 26)
58%	How satisfied are you with your involvement in decisions that affect your work? (Q. 33)
58%	How satisfied are you with the information you receive from management on what's going on in your organization? (Q. 34)
59%	How satisfied are you with the recognition you receive for doing a good job? (Q. 35)
60%	Managers promote communication among different work units (for example, about projects, goals, needed resources). (Q. 29)
61%	My organization's senior leaders maintain high standards of honesty and integrity. (Q. 27)
62%	I have a high level of respect for my organization's senior leaders. (Q. 31)

- become better listeners
- ask questions in a curious way
- set judgment aside
- develop compassion and empathy
- learn to appreciate the person in front of them

Leaders who possess and use these skills are effectively *better* leaders. They can handle conversations more effectively, including more difficult ones. In fact, they might even explore what is driving the results of FEVS. They are more likely to make time for conversations with employees at crucial junctions, such as to discuss individual development plans and performance appraisals. When employees have positive experiences with leaders who are good listeners, non-judgmental, and allow them to share freely, trust can grow in the relationship. M. Johnson shared, "In the federal space, a lot of it comes down to power dynamics and an individual's ability to access their own power. How does a leader activate that power in others?" Leaders have positional power, and they have an opportunity to enable the power of others in the workplace. From their positions of power, leaders can use their coaching skills to engage with their direct reports and help them be successful in their current roles and support their professional development and advancement. More of these kinds of leadership behaviors would likely positively impact employees' relations with both leaders and FEVS results.

Four Changes to Make in Government

Our interviewees agreed with four changes to make in the federal government that would help achieve a coaching culture.

1. **Create a job series for coaches**. As of this writing, coaching is not a profession in the U.S. Federal Government Handbook of Occupational Groups and Families. Consequently, no one in the federal government is a full-time coach. We recommend OPM create a job series for full-time professional coach positions. A job series would permit organizations to staff professional coaches.
2. **Continue to train internal employees to coach on a part-time basis**. Having a volunteer cadre of part-time coaches creates the opportunity for any employee to receive coaching. Look for programs with DEIA as a foundation or as an integrated component.
3. **Develop a government-wide policy for coaching**. Such a policy would allow employees to confidently request coaching and supervisors to support coaching. It would support part-time coaches to coach during duty hours and would authorize supervisors to grant permission.
4. **Train coach-like basic skills to all employees, managers, and SES**. Embedding coach-like skills with all roles and processes enables organizations to build a culture of coaching. Training must also include modules on unconscious bias and power dynamics to help participants become more self-aware.

Although the number of trained coaches is increasing in the federal government, it will take years to reach critical mass. We believe there should be increased funding for both certified coach development training programs and an expansion of the application of coach-like skills in the workplace. If the federal government did this, other organizations both public and private in the United States and in other countries may follow suit. The more that coaching and coach-like skills are integrated into our daily communications and interactions, the more we will listen to each other with curiosity, compassion, and empathy. Tolerance for differing perspectives and beliefs is likely to follow, allowing for sharing, appreciation, and understanding.

We conclude with a new appreciation for coaching and the ways the federal government can use it to address current challenges. Learning to be a coach is a transformational skill for work and life and a powerful way of being with the potential to change the workplace.

Key Takeaways

- With a cadre of trained coaches, who are ready and willing to serve, we have an opportunity to use coaching as a tool for change.
- When the federal government senior leaders, managers, and employees use coach-like skills, the very culture of government can change.
- Coaching has the potential to have the greatest impact on DEIA and belonging as those with coach-like skills can express empathy, compassion, and appreciation for others, including their employees.
- Applying coach-like skills throughout all levels of leadership and management is one tangible step that agencies could take to impact the low ratings in the FEVS.
- Changes that need to be made in government to better support the coaching movement are create a job series for coaches, continue to train internal employees to coach on a part-time basis, develop a government-wide policy for coaching, and train basic coach-like skills to all employees, managers, and SES.

Key Questions

- How can you utilize your coaching cadre within your own agency to support mission success?
- How is your agency addressing DEIA and belonging? How can coaching be built into the strategy?
- How does your agency develop leaders? How can coaching be integrated into the leader development strategy?

References

Barta, T., Kleiner, M., & Newman, T. (2012, April 1). Is there a payoff from top-team diversity? *McKinsey and Company, McKinsey Quarterly.* https://www.mckinsey.com/business-functions/people-and-organizational-performance/our-insights/is-there-a-payoff-from-top-team-diversity

Exec. Order No. 14,035, 3 C.F.R. 34,953 (2021). https://www.federalregister.gov/d/2021-14127

Garvey Berger, J. (2019). *Unlocking leadership mindtraps: How to thrive in complexity.* Stanford University Press.

Imperial College London. (n.d.). Unconscious bias. Retrieved January 1, 2022, from https://www.imperial.ac.uk/equality/resources/unconscious-bias/

Lardy, B. (2021, August 26). A revealing look at racial diversity in the federal government. *Partnership for Public Service. We the Partnership, Diversity, Equity and Inclusion.* https://ourpublicservice.org/blog/a-revealing-look-at-racial-diversity-in-the-federal-government/

U.S. Office of Personnel Management. (2020). *Federal employee viewpoint survey empowering employees empowering change* [Governmentwide Management Report]. https://www.opm.gov/fevs/reports/governmentwide-reports/governmentwide-management-report/governmentwide-report/2020/2020-governmentwide-management-report.pdf

Appendix 1: Tributes to Coaching Pioneers

Through our work to document the history of coaching in the federal government, we identified and talked with many early adopters who established coaching practices and programs before they became prevalent. A few stood out and we wanted to recognize their unique contributions. We invite you to learn more about each of these pioneers highlighted in the book.

Alan Lee Myers, PCC

Cassandra Brennand

Cheri Allen, PCC

Gordon Lee Salmon (deceased)

Larry Westberg

Lynne (Marilyn Nancy) Feingold, PCC

Randy Bergquist, M.S.

Richard Donald Hansen, Jr.

Dr. Juanita (Sue) Stein, EdD, PCC

We do this with the understanding that there are too many people to name, countless who contributed in small but mighty ways to the creation of coaching in federal government and should not be forgotten. Many unsung heroes—including supervisors, friends, and family of federal employees—brought coaching and much more to their workplaces.

Other Notable Trailblazers:

Matilda Broadnax, first FICTP graduate to become an ACC

Judith Diaz Myers, first FICTP graduate to become a PCC

Michelle Reugebrink, first active civil servant to become an MCC

Alan Lee Myers, PCC

Serves in the U.S. Federal Food and Drug Administration. Previously served in the Office of the Secretary, HHS, Centers for Medicare and Medicaid Services, Indian Health Service, Office of Personnel Management, Federal Communications Commission, and the Federal Energy Regulatory Commission.

Alan Lee Myers, PCC

How Were You Drawn to Coaching?

A lot of people were drawn to coaching because of an experience with a coach. Mine wasn't that way, it was more a function of necessity. I received my master's degree in counseling, so I really had at least the basic skills of listening and questioning. You already know all the things they teach you in coaching school to be an effective coach, but it was more therapeutic in nature and more crisis or crisis oriented. When I began my career in the federal government, I was exposed to career counseling. It benefits the clients but it really didn't hit me until several years into my federal career, when I started working for the Indian Health Service (IHS). The IHS director would tell his new executives who came from tribal organizations and private industry to come talk to me. So, new execs would knock on the door occasionally. I would say the "doctor's in, have a seat" and that's literally how my career started in coaching. And I didn't even call it that. The only thing I knew was how to be an effective therapist. I just knew positive regard, you know, active listening, and asking powerful questions. They didn't call it coaching back then. So, I was just doing what I knew and what I was trained to do.

How Did You Learn to Coach?

I explored New Ventures West in the mid-nineties, but I couldn't get the funding, around $8,000 at the time. So, I spent about ten years reading coaching books and getting exposed to coaching while continuing my leadership development work and doing O.D. consulting. Then, when I was at CMS, they used end of year funding so I could attend the Georgetown University Leadership Coaching Program in 2004–2005. I was just in the right place at the right time. When I went through the program, I said, "Oh wow, I've been doing it right." Then, I also learned, "Therapy is not it, right?" What was missing for me was the sense of getting a really solid agreement and also the sense of, okay, how do I manage progress?

What Are You Known for in the Government Coaching World?

I think probably what I'm known for even in some of my O.D. work is, I'm the guy who if you tell me something can't be done, I'll figure out a way you get it done. Give me a challenge and I'll figure out a way. I am specifically known for getting federal employees to coach other federal employees and training people to coach. Is that an original idea? No, because other people have done it in other governments around the world, the National Health System in Great Britain and they've been doing it longer than me for sure. But I think I'm probably the first one who said, "Hey we don't need contractors to do this, we can do it on our own."

What Is Your Favorite Coaching Moment?

I have many favorites. Without violating confidences, a senior leader in a former organization got involved in a particularly sticky political issue. The president at the time had promised a certain thing but the reality was that this individual had to say, "No we can't do that." And he was a senior official. He was put under a situation of severe political pressure by the administration. That particular situation wasn't unique to senior executives, so I enrolled him in the coaching process. He understood the process and I was able to help him rethink and reframe the situation. That was probably my favorite because of the work I did with him. He became a well-known and well-respected individual in the organization and in his profession worldwide. As a result of this coaching engagement, I worked with all his managers in a team coaching arrangement.

Cassandra Brennand

Served in the Office of Personnel Management.

Cassandra Brennand

How Were You Drawn To Coaching?

One of the very first projects of my federal career with OPM was to create an Executive Development Best Practices Guide, which was released in November 2012. As part of that research, I conducted several in-depth interviews with learning leaders across a variety of Fortune 500 organizations and federal agencies. This research illuminated a significant difference in approach to executive coaching by private and public sectors—federal agencies tended to use coaching to remedy poor performance versus a holistic development opportunity (often paired with assessments) in the private industry. My curiosity was piqued enough to begin learning more about coaching and seeking out instances of coaching practice within government—which ultimately led me to Alan Myers at HHS who was piloting a Federal Coaching Boot Camp training program for internal coaches. I participated in his program in 2014, and we partnered closely to establish and build the government-wide Federal Coaching Network and Internal Training Program over the next few years.

How Did You Learn To Coach?

My introduction to coaching happened through Alan's first HHS Coaching Program, and I subsequently served as a mentor coach in future iterations of FICTP. From there, I went on to earn a few different coaching and assessment certifications, including NeuroLeadership Institute's Brain-Based Coaching Certificate, GLP Coaching Certificate, Leadership Circle Profile, and Immunity to Change.

What Are You Known for in the Government Coaching World?

I like to think of myself as being in the right role, at the right time, with the right kind of support to create space and a platform for coaching to step into the spotlight in the federal government. Pockets of coaching practice had existed, and incredible people in different roles across agencies had such passion, skill, energy, and commitment to the power of coaching—I was able to bring them all together in service of a greater vision and bring coaching to life and scale it across the federal government. The mission of FCN was uniquely designed as a triple win—a win for coaches who could engage in coaching and training as part of their jobs, a win for coachees across government who gained access to a tremendous developmental resource at no cost, and a win for government overall by building developmental networks, coaching capability, and increased employee engagement across agencies.

Cheri Allen, PCC

Serves in the Internal Revenue Service. Previously served at Veterans Administration, Peace Corps, Department of Education, Federal Emergency Management Agency, Government Printing Office, Treasury Departmental Offices, and Homeland Security.

Cheri Allen, PCC

How Were You Drawn to Coaching?

When I served at the U.S. Department of Education (DOE), I completed a detail in the Training and Development Office where I was asked to revamp the coaching program. In order to authentically market the program, I asked to receive a coach to experience what being coached was like. Although as a GS-13 employee I did not meet the requirements of being a team leader, supervisor, manager, or executive, my request was granted because I was a program manager. The experience was transformational on so many levels—professionally and personally, and I still benefit today from what I learned about myself back in the year 2000!

What Are You Known for in the Government Coaching World?

I am a *Coaching Influencer & Strategist*. More specifically, I am known for being one of the pioneers who provided coaching in the federal government. In 2005, *The Government Training News* published an article about the DOE's "novel coaching program" that provided coaching to leaders in the organization. In addition, that same year I was invited to present at an Excellence in Government conference and an American University event about how I aligned coaching with the organization's strategic goals and the Executive Core Qualifications. I am one of the founding champions of FICTP and I continue to serve on the Governance Board for Federal Internal Coaching and as a faculty member and mentor coach to coaches-in-training across the federal government.

What Is Your Favorite Coaching Moment?

My favorite coaching moment is when my coach asked me in a moment of being stuck, "Cheri, what is it going to take to get your mojo back?" Well, that question got me unstuck and still drives me to this very day. I live in the place of infinite possibilities, and I have found my ALIVENESS pursuing them!

Gordon Lee Salmon (deceased)

Served at Department of Interior, National Business Center, Department of Treasury: Federal Consulting Group (FCG), and the Environmental Protection Agency.

Gordon Lee Salmon

We were unable to interview Lee Salmon and created his tribute based on his writings and interviews with those who knew him.

Gordon "Lee" Salmon moved to the Washington, DC, area in 1988 to work at EPA as a health physicist. In 1996, he graduated from the Newfield Network Coaching Program, which changed his life in a substantial way. He was passionate about bringing coaching to the federal government and using coaching as a way to protect the earth's environment. He believed that coaching conversations would not only transform individuals and organizations, but also the planet. He was an avid champion for leadership and self-development, which led him to find a place at the Federal Consulting Group (FCG), where he served as its Coaching Program Practice Manager. In this role, he provided coaching and consulting services to federal agencies. FCG had a cadre of contract coaches and Lee offered his coaching services to executives. In this role, he offered periodic meetings for both his cadre of coaches and clients. He was the consummate networker and facilitator. Everyone who knew Lee always spoke highly of his quiet, generous, gregarious, and jovial demeanor. He never spoke ill of anyone. He loved people and held parties where people from different walks of life met and connected. Many people owe their coaching career journeys to Lee. He always celebrated other coach's success, especially in the federal government.

Lee was a member of the Board of Directors, International Consortium for Coaching in Organizations. He retired from the federal government in 2010 and continued to coach in private practice until his passing in 2014. An award was established in his name, The Gordon Lee Salmon Sustainable Leadership Award, by the Library of Professional Coaching. Lee authored a few articles; the following is from *Coaching and Transformational Listening*:

> At times in a coaching relationship, the client and coach experience a deep listening that creates a powerful sense of trust....Listening and silence are the twins of being; they create and maintain this ritual space. Silence is so rich with possibilities; it is where we can meet, connect, and dance with life.
>
> (Salmon, 2002, pp. 58–60)[1]

This quote sums up how Lee lived his life.

Larry Westberg

Served in the Department of Defense.

Larry Westberg

How Were You Drawn to Coaching?

My first duties back at DoD were various educational responsibilities with the Defense Senior Leader Development Program (DSLDP), including managing four contract coaches for our senior leaders. Although each coach was very different in personality and background, I sensed an attractive air of confidence and presence in all the coaches, which made me want to find out more about coaching. My boss at the time, Dr. Sue Stein, was already researching private coach training programs. Soon, we had a small cohort that started formal coach training with the Center for Executive Coaching headed by Andrew Neitlich, with mentor coach Barbara Hulick.

How Did You Learn to Coach?

I first started learning by observing great coaches at work. This was followed up with formal coach training at the Center for Executive Coaching and lots and lots of practice with great clients. Marshall Goldsmith is correct when he said "Highly motivated clients make the best coaches!"

What Are You Known for in the Government Coaching World?

I am probably best known as a networker of coaches. I was one of the founders of FCN, a voluntary group of federal internal coaches who provide coaching, coach training, and learning experiences throughout the Federal Enterprise. With Dr. Sue Stein, Lee Salmon, Ed Mosley, and Richard Hansen, I helped start the Government Community of Practice with the ICF Maryland and ICF Metro Washington DC chapters. Within DoD, I am known for recruiting motivated clients for my fellow internal coaches. My greatest joy today is helping a wide variety of people realize their dream of becoming a coach.

Lynne (Marilyn Nancy) Feingold, PCC

Previously served at Internal Revenue Service, National Endowment for the Arts, Fiscal Service, GSA, Department of Treasury, TEI, Department of State, DHS (USCIS), and IRS.

Lynne Feingold, PCC

How Were You Drawn to Coaching?

In the second grade, I told my teacher I wanted everyone to work on a project together where everyone could be their best and could help everyone to be their best. The teacher said that it is a great goal but I would have to wait until I was an adult, and I replied immediately, "But I don't want to wait!" She didn't even reply! Looking back, I was asking her to be a coach and allow the students to do peer coaching. Then, in the fourth grade, I took up flute and played in a band, continued with piano, and later took up voice. So, I naturally hear what we say in everyday conversation—the words and sentences—like notes in music. Communication has the characteristics of music—tempo, pitch, phrasing, sensation, and feeling. I've always been drawn to deep listening, which both musicians and coaches must have.

What Are You Known for in the Government Coaching World?

I'm known as a visionary who had a dream of a government-wide coaching culture—a nearly inconceivable idea at the time. Looking back, it was my second-grade story that guided my vision. I wanted people's best selves to be seen and heard. I'm told by clients that I challenge them with a safety net. I help them get comfortable with what's not naturally comfortable. I take clients to *their* highest peak on the mountain.

What Is Your Favorite Coaching Moment?

An executive who traveled extensively with a former secretary of one of the major departments in government came to coaching, wanting someone to tell her what she should do for the next step of her career. At the end of the six-month coaching engagement, we reviewed her initial goals and where she was. She said with delight, "I came to coaching wanting *someone* to tell me what to do with my career. I found that someone. *It's me.*"

Randy Bergquist, M.S.

Previously served Department of Justice, Department of Homeland Security, Department of Transportation, and Department of Commerce.

Randy Bergquist, M.S.

How Were You Drawn to Coaching?

While studying music during my undergraduate years, I served as a peer counselor in the residence halls. This opportunity sparked my interest to help young adults manage a variety of challenges. This experience led me to earn a master's degree in counseling. While in graduate school, I continued to apply my coaching and counseling skills as a residence hall director, where I trained and led a staff of resident hall peer counselors. After graduate school, the Catholic University of America hired me to serve as the Assistant Director of Housing, where I was a counselor and trainer for resident hall life. After one year in this position, I pursued a career in the federal government as an employee development specialist. Over a 36-year career in the federal government, I served in employee development and employee relations specialist positions. While in these positions, I continued to use my coaching and counseling skills to help hundreds of employees with their personal and professional skill development, as well as coaching all levels of leadership with their staff-related learning and development activities.

What Are You Known for in the Government Coaching World?

As an employee development specialist for four cabinet-level agencies, I coached hundreds of employees at all levels for the purpose of career and professional development. Between 2010 and 2016, while serving as Chair of the CLOC, in partnership with OPM, I led several high-level federal learning and development initiatives, including designing, developing, and implementing FCN. Since 2013, over 500 federal coaches have been trained and invested in the practice of coaching.

What Is Your Favorite Coaching Moment?

Having coached for over four decades, it's hard to identify one favorite moment. Each time I'm given the opportunity to help others explore options for moving from a current state to a desired state of personal and professional wellness, it brings me deep joy and happiness. Even more exciting is when those I've mentored have become certified coaches, both in the public and private sectors.

Richard Donald Hansen, Jr.

Serves in the Defense Acquisition University. Previous served at the Department of Defense.

Richard Donald Hansen, Jr

How Were You Drawn to Coaching?

As I was nearing my Army retirement in 2008, I was contemplating the next phase of my employment and career. I can't remember how I learned of coaching, but I did, and it sounded like a possible avenue for me and a way to continue to be in service to others. I had also considered applying to be a faculty member at DAU to serve as a government consultant and give back to the defense acquisition workforce. As I explored this avenue, I learned that DAU was thinking about starting up an executive coaching service for high-level, large-portfolio program managers. That combination of faculty and consultant and the ability to coach sealed the deal for me.

How Did You Learn to Coach?

As part of starting up the coaching practice at DAU, we hired executive coach and author Robert Hargrove to teach us his Masterful Coaching approach. He was the executive coach to the HON John Young from his days as the Navy's Service Acquisition Executive and his accession to the Undersecretary of Defense for Acquisition, Training, and Logistics. HON Young's successful experience with coaching led him to direct DAU to train some coaches and offer them to the ACAT 1D Program Managers. A couple of years later, I enrolled initially in an ICF-credentialed training, Presence-Based Coaching for my ACSTH, then, subsequently participated in their Living in Presence Coaching Course (ACTP). My learning of coaching accelerated when we decided to "make not buy" our own training (a decade of training our own coaches) and I became the lead for coaching enterprise at DAU.

What Are You Known for in the Government Coaching World?

I am known for coaching key leaders in the defense acquisition workforce, who lead large, integrated teams and organizations that develop, acquire, and sustain operational capability for the DoD and its military services. These key leaders are professionals in the fields of program management, contracting, life cycle logistics, engineering and technical management, test and evaluation, and business—financial management. At DAU, we offer these key leaders a six-step model that includes: designing and implementing an extraordinary future, charting and engaging stakeholders, and conducting an executive (360) feedback.

Dr. Juanita (Sue) Stein, EdD, PCC

Served Department of the Interior: National Park Service; U.S. Department of Agriculture: Cooperative Extension Service; Department of Defense: U.S. Army, Defense Acquisition University, the Washington Headquarters Services, the Defense Logistics Agency and the Civilian Personnel Management Service.

How Did You Learn to Coach?

I was introduced to basic coaching skills as part of the training for various leadership assessment certifications that I completed. From there, I became

Dr. Sue Stein, EdD, PCC

interested in how I could improve my coaching for professionals, both at their work and life generally.

It was not until I worked at the Pentagon and was the lead for contracting for external coaches that I was able to propose and secure funding for one of the first groups of internal government staff to be formally trained as coaches under an ICF-accredited coaching program. At that point, I and several of my peers were selected for the internal coach training program that I helped launch in DoD. From that point on, I have spent time and resources on expanding my coaching skills annually.

What Are You Known for in the Government Coaching World?

I am known for having the vision to start and launch several initiatives for government coaching. For example, I was a part of the cross-government Coaching Consortium when L Feingold at TEI wanted to start an internal group for government coaches.

When I left full-time government, I conceived the idea of a special interest group (SIG) for government as part of ICF Global. The first group became the ICF Metro Government Coaching Community of Practice, going strong currently under the leadership of L. Westberg.

Other more recent coaching projects I am known for include: the University of Government Coaching (an ICF-accredited curriculum for coaches interested in government); the Coaching Leads Project (a by-invitation group dedicated to securing external coaching opportunities to support government); the Volunteers for Government Coaching Research (a group of volunteer coaches interested in conducing survey research on challenges, trends and effective practices in government coaching); and the Friends of Government Coaching News (a newsletter for leaders of groups of government coaches).

What Is Your Favorite Coaching Moment?

After more than 20 years as a coach, the favorite coaching moments are too numerous to recount. It always warms my heart when someone tells me my coaching has made a true difference in their life.

Note

1   The quote by G. Lee Salmon is from the article he wrote for *Coaching with spirit* and has been reprinted with permission of the author, T. Belf. The reference is listed in Chapter 1.

Appendix 2: Tools and Templates

Program managers should establish documents and forms needed to support their programs, clients, and coaches. Taking the time to assess the needs of the program and prepare the documents before the launch allows the program to have a professional start.

This Appendix provides a variety of samples and templates that can be adapted for individual coaching programs. Remember to brand and have a consistent look and feel for the program materials as well as obtain any necessary legal reviews.

Tool	Page	Purpose
Policy Document Template	154	Policies provide needed governance and establish credibility in organizations. The document can be used to build a coaching policy.
Coaching SOP Template	158	Standard operating procedures (SoPs) provide guidance for daily tasks in a program. This document can be adapted to create SoPs for a coaching program.
Coaching Frequently Asked Questions Sample	176	Program managers must be able to provide consistent answers to frequently asked questions. This document provides some frequently asked questions and sample answers.

Tool	Page	Purpose
Sample Join Coach Cadre Form	182	Recruiting coaches for a new or ongoing program is a necessity. This form collects the basic information from a coach interested in joining a cadre.
Coach Bio Template	183	Program managers need to know their coaches. A standard bio allows them to collect information for their reference. This document may also be used with clients.
Sample Coach Development Plan	184	Coaches love to continue their development. This document allows coaches to reflect on and plan to develop both their coaching and leadership skills.
Sample Coach Request	186	Program managers must have the client's information to make a match. This document is a sample for the client request.
Sample Intake Session Outline	187	There is much to cover during an intake session, when the coach and client meet for the first time. This outline provides a structure to share with coaches so consistent information is shared with every client.
Sample Coaching Agreement	189	A coaching agreement helps the coach and client co-create their relationship and provides clarity around roles, responsibilities and is the foundation for the relationship. This is a sample coaching agreement used at the DIA. Remember to have coaching agreements reviewed by the legal department before using.
Sample Assignment Emails	193	Communications from the program manager and coach after a request should be professional and provide information. These samples can be used to develop your initial assignment email templates.
Sample Assignment Check-in Emails	195	Once the coach is assigned, the program manager generally does not hear back until the end of the engagement. This check-in email (or a similar one) can be sent several weeks after the initial session to see that all is well.
Sample Coach Reflection Form	196	Helping the coach reflect on their coaching is key to improving skills. This document can be shared with coaches to use at the end of a session or an assignment.

Tool	Page	Purpose
Sample Coaching Evaluation Questions	197	Evaluating coaching is essential to maintaining and improving programs. This document provides some sample questions to consider when you are developing a coaching evaluation.
Sample End of Coaching Engagement Survey	198	This is a sample coaching evaluation survey that can be adapted for use in a coaching program.
Sample Impact I Survey	201	This survey was designed to measure the leadership effectiveness of leaders who become certified coaches. It focuses on workplace relationships.
Sample Impact Survey II	204	This survey makes Impact Survey I a 360-degree view of the impact of coaching by asking those in a coach's workplace about behaviors of the leader before and after they became a certified coach.

Policy Document Template

Use this template as a starting point to develop an official internal policy for an internal coaching program.

- PURPOSE: Establishes policy and assigned responsibilities for the [your organization name] Coaching Program as a leadership development and performance improvement tool authorized in accordance with (IAW) Reference [list any references] which ensures the development and retention of a motivated and productive workforce for the successful execution of [your organization name's] mission.
- The Coaching Program is designed to support broad training objectives that will improve and enhance productivity and performance, foster continuous personal and professional growth, and create an environment of learning, throughout [your organization name] workforce. Coaching is a critical augmentation to training, leadership development, and performance improvement. [YOUR ORGANIZATION NAME] personnel will have opportunities to coach other employees and receive coaching from qualified [YOUR ORGANIZATION NAME] coaches. [YOUR ORGANIZATION NAME] supports coaching as a learning method and endorses activities, training, and communications leading to the establishment of coaching relationships.

References

- List any policies or directives that support this policy

Applicability

- What is the population to whom this policy applies? Is the entire organization? Are there any excluded populations?

Roles and responsibilities

- List all who have a role with respect to this program and what they are designated to be responsible for.
- The Training Organization of [your organization name] will:
  - Implement and maintain oversight of the Coach Certification Program.

- Develop and administer training course to develop certified coaches.
- Maintain a list of certified coaches.
- Provide ongoing support, mentorship, and learning opportunities to Certified Coaches as part of certification requirements.

- Certified Coaches will:

  - Complete the coach certification course through training offered by [your organization name] or verify prior certification by submitting certificates of other coach certification programs to the coaching program manager.
  - Conduct coaching activities as a collateral duty, during normal working hours, with permission of the supervisor.
  - Establish a formal coaching agreement and relationship with the client
  - Only engage in formal coaching relationships with employees outside my current chain of command
  - Adhere to federal principles of conduct and the [identify a coach credentialing association] code of coaching professional ethics.
  - Take appropriate action with [your organization name] authorities to address any ethics violation or possible breach as soon as I become aware.
  - Report knowledge of any professional or personal misconduct to the appropriate [your organization name] authorities.

- Supervisors must authorize personnel who are certified coaches to conduct coaching as part of their regular duty hours, when mission demands permit.

Procedures

- [your organization name] Certified Coaches attain Coach certification by:

  - Successfully completing the [your organization name] Coach Certification Program.
  - Submitting certificates or documentation showing completion of an approved coach certification program.

- Certified Coaches maintain coach certification by completing and submitting annual requirements, a coaching log, to the coaching program manager showing documented hours of coaching and certificates of completion for coach-related training events.

- Annual requirements include 1–3 hours of coaching activities (see definitions) per week or a minimum of 24 hours of coaching per year as well as three coaching-related continuous learning opportunities specified by the coaching program manager.

  - Coaches may be assigned to clients through referral from other employees, on their own, and through a central coach enrollment process managed by the coaching program manager.
  - Coaches will perform coaching during normal duty hours with approval of their supervisor.
  - Coaches requiring additional support concerning ethical dilemmas or questionable behavior may reach out to the coaching program manager.

- [your organization name] Employees:

  - Select a coach from the approved coach pool or work with a coach if participating in a formal organization learning program where a coach is assigned.
  - Personnel who seek coaching will sign and adhere to a written coaching agreement that describes the terms of the coaching agreement.
  - Personnel must initiate and maintain reasonable contact with the coach and attend coaching sessions.

- [your organization name] Supervisors:

  - Refer personnel seeking coaching to the Coaching Program.
  - Refer personnel seeking the opportunity to become a certified coach to the coaching program manager.

Definitions

- Certified Coach—An individual who has completed all of the requirements of an International Coach Federation (or equivalent) approved or accredited coach training certification program.
- Coaching client—One who seeks the support and skills of a coach. In an organizational setting, the coaching client is the person who is receiving the coaching. (client, coachee, and coaching client are used interchangeably.)

- Coach (or professional coach)—A qualified professional who works with clients to improve their effectiveness and performance and helps them achieve their full potential. A coach offers support, skills, and honest feedback in service of the client.
- Coachee / client—The person who is being coached.
- Coaching activities—These activities include conducting or receiving coaching in person, on the telephone, or through other conferencing approaches. Activities also include events offered for training or continuous learning purposes.
- Coach in training (CIT)—Someone enrolled in coach training.
- Coaching—A creative process that inspires "clients" to maximize their personal and professional potential. Coaching is a distinct service and differs greatly from counseling, mentoring, or training.
- Coach Mentor—A qualified professional who focuses on the ongoing development of coaching skills in support of coaches.
- Coaching supervision—Interaction that occurs when a coach periodically brings his or her coaching work experiences to a Coaching Supervisor in order to engage in reflective dialogue and collaborative learning for the development and benefit of the coach and his or her clients.
- Formal coaching—When a trained and certified coach engages in a relationship with a client using a formal coaching agreement, utilizing core coaching competencies and skills, demonstrating confidentiality, and ethical behaviors.
- Professional coaching relationship—A confidential coaching relationship that includes a written agreement that defines the responsibilities of both parties.

Code of Ethics

Coaching SOP Template

Table of Contents

Version History

Reviews of this SOP are conducted semi-annually. Substantial programmatic updates will be detailed in enclosures, noted in the "Description" column below; updates will be detailed in an enclosure if they cannot be described in full below.

Version	Date	Author	Description

Definitions

Client: An individual who collaborates with a coach to maximize performance potential.

Coaching: In the federal government, it is defined as *a collaborative, results-driven development process that inspires people to maximize their performance potential. (As per OPM Memo on Coaching)*

Coaching Agreement: A guiding document that outlines the parameters of the coaching relationship and defines the specific roles and responsibilities of each party invested in the coaching outcome.

Coaching Engagement: When a coach meets a client for the first time, an overall plan for coaching is made. Together, all the meetings make up a Coaching Engagement.

Coach Mentor: Coach Mentors are Certified Coaches who have received additional training that allows them to provide specific feedback to Certified Coaches on their coaching competencies.

Coaching Supervisor: A trained and accredited experienced coach who provides collaborative learning practice to continually build the capacity of the coach through reflective dialogue for the benefit of both coaches and clients.

External Coach: A professional coach, who is either self-employed or partners with other professional coaches to provide coaching services to the Government.

Internal Federal Coach: A professional certified coach, who is employed within a federal agency and provides coaching services to other federal employees in their own agencies and across the Government.

Leader as Coach: A leader who leverages coaching knowledge, approaches, and techniques in working with their employees to maximize performance potential.

Professional Coach: An individual who offers support to others through a mutual partnership designed to maximize performance potential. A professional coaching relationship exists to meet the needs of individuals or teams and must be guided by a written coaching agreement.

Overview of Coaching at

Purpose

The goal of the Coaching Program is to provide all employees at all grade levels with access to an internal coach in order to increase transfer of learning, create a positive and supportive organizational culture, and promote personal self-awareness for professional growth.

This standard operating procedure codifies the [name] Coaching Program, managed by the [ ]. This standard operating procedure (SOP) reflects guidance from [your policy]. It contains the services and procedures supported by the Coaching Program and provides the specific requirements and responsibilities for becoming and maintaining the status of one's Coach Certification.

Standards

Coaching and being coached are both authorized by [your document]. On September 10, 2018, the director of OPM issued a memo to agency leaders highlighting the "importance of creating a coaching culture." (see https://chcoc.gov/content/coaching-federal-government)

In addition, Coaching is a sanctioned learning and development experience cited in the regulatory requirements surrounding training (5 CFR 410.203) and succession management (5 CFR 412.201). 5 CFR 412.202 also requires agencies to provide training to supervisors, managers, and executives on improving employee performance and productivity. Equipping leaders with coaching skills is a proven and effective way to enhance employee development and performance.

General Overview

• [Provide an overview of your program]

Defining Coaching

Coaching is defined by the International Coach Federation (ICF) as "partnering with clients in a thought-provoking and creative process that inspires them to maximize their personal and professional potential."

Coaching in the federal government is recognized by the Office of Personnel Management (OPM) as a collaborative, results-driven development process that inspires people to maximize their performance potential. (Federal Coaching Network and OPM definition). "Coaching is a critical tool as the Federal Government strives to develop a workforce that supports the effective and efficient mission achievement and improved services to the American people." (Dr. Jeff T.H. Pon, OPM)

Whether it is learning to be a coach, being coached, or demonstrating coach-like behaviors in the workplace, coaching in any capacity is considered professional development for internal coach, client, and leader, and often leads to a positive performance outcome. As any other authorized development activity, time spent in professional coaching, as an internal federal coach or client, must be approved by the employee's supervisor with consideration to organizational priorities.

Coaching within the government is also intentionally applied to learning opportunities within Leadership Development programs.

Oversight/Ethical Standards

Standards of coaching are defined by professional coaching organizations such as the International Coaching Federation (ICF). The practice of coaching is unregulated. However, ICF does provide a Code of Ethics, which all coaches are required to follow. Federal internal coaches are bound to uphold the basic obligation for public service and the standards for ethical conduct for federal employees found in 5 CFR Part 2635. These standards supersede any and all coach-specific code of ethics and must be addressed appropriately in the Coaching Agreement, specifically the limits of confidentiality and conflicts of interest.

A Coaching Code of Ethics was developed with elements of 5 CFR Part 2635 and the International Coach Federation Coaching Code of Ethics.

Approved Coaching Agreement

A professional coaching relationship includes an agreement that outlines the parameters of the coaching relationship and defines the specific roles and responsibilities of each party (coach and client) invested in the coaching outcome. [your organization name] requires Coaches to use an approved coaching agreement by the second meeting with the client. The approved Coaching Agreement can be found [here].

Confidentiality

All information discussed during a coaching engagement is confidential unless the client gives explicit permission to share information, or it is required by law to report something. [You organization name] requires Coaches to use an approved coaching agreement, which includes a statement of confidentiality. The Coaching Agreement describes that confidentiality is not protected in the same way as doctor/patient, lawyer/client agreements. Limits of confidentiality in the federal government include a report of an act of fraud, waste or abuse; the revelation of having committed a crime; the threat of harm to self or others; the sharing of information in violation of a security clearance; the report of sexual harassment; the requirement by law or a court order to share particular information.

Coaching Engagements

Individuals may engage in coaching for a variety of reasons related to maximizing performance. Examples of potential coaching objectives include the following:

- Maximize onboarding of new leaders
- Develop leadership skills of technical experts

- Facilitate personal or professional transitions
- Organize and prioritize professional responsibilities
- Clarify vision, create meaningful goals, and develop achievable action steps
- Facilitate change management
- Achieve professional goals
- Streamline or identify functional efficiencies
- Solve individual leadership or other challenges
- Excel in accountability, self-awareness, and self-management
- Identify core strengths and recognize how best to leverage them
- Gain clarity in purpose and decision making
- Identify values and examine how they are or are not modeled in behaviors and actions
- Improve professional relationships

The Benefits of Coaching

Coaching offers many benefits to the individual being coached as well as to the organization as a whole. In a coaching relationship, the client benefits from one-on-one interaction and feedback focused exclusively on their own goals and development. In the case of [your agency name], the overall goal is to foster and improve learning, development, and discovery among all employees at any time in their professional life or, specifically, when implementing practices from the Officer Development programs. Topic areas can range from career development to improving communication skills to resolving a workplace challenge or conflict.

Benefits to the individual include:

- New perspectives on personal or organizational challenges
- Improvements in individual performance goals and targets
- Increased self-awareness
- Greater clarity of roles and responsibilities
- Improvements in specific skills or behaviors
- Increased confidence and self-motivation
- Greater work and life satisfaction

Benefits to the organization include:

- Improved use of individual's talents and potential
- Commitment to individuals and their development

- Higher organizational performance and productivity
- Honed focus on mission and organizational objectives
- Increased creativity, learning, and knowledge
- Improved relationships between people and organizations

How Coaching Enhances the Leadership Development

The Coaching Program is integrated in the Leadership Development curriculum, serving as a powerful new tool for enhanced learning and development for every leader. Previously, coaching was something available only to employees in the senior ranks of the organization as part of their learning and development programs.

The Leadership Development Program is supercharged through coaching:

- Learning: When coupled with formal learning, coaching increases learning by 80%.
- Development: Employees accelerate their capabilities by working on areas identified in behavioral assessments as part of their program.
- Discovery: Through coaching, employees discover new perspectives and courses of action to tackle similar problems.

Processes of Becoming a Coach

Becoming a Certified Coach begins with the individual completing a professional coach training program. [Describe what is involved in becoming a coach at your organization]

Eligibility and Enrollment

General eligibility requirements include [adapt to reflect your organization's eligibility criteria]:

- A minimum of two years employment with [your organization]
- Has not had an EO complaints, disciplinary, misconduct, deficient performance or other grievances lodged against him/her in the last two years
- Received appraisal scores of "Successful" or higher each of the last two years

Applicants complete the application with a compelling rationale for their interest in becoming a Certified Coach.

After completing the application, the participant will route the application to their supervisor. The supervisor reviews the application and attests the eligibility requirements. The supervisor is allowed to veto the application for any reason pertaining to the employee's performance or mission requirements.

Applications are reviewed by committee and initially prioritized in order of receipt for those who have completed the registration, the application, and the Supervisor's approval. Care is put into putting a mixture of participants from different grades, locations, and organizations.

Sessions between Coach and Client

Typically, the coach and client will meet in person or on the telephone to become acquainted, to discuss the goals for coaching, and to set up a time for a first meeting. During the first meeting, the overall goal of the coaching relationship is typically discussed and the coaching agreement for a set period is reviewed and signed. A signed agreement should be in the hands of the client and the coach by the second coaching meeting. Subsequent sessions are related to the overall goal. Within the sessions, the coach will ask the client questions that will evoke awareness surrounding the issue, situation, or goal the client has identified. The coach will explore options the client can consider. The session typically ends with an action or an inquiry that the client commits to pursue for the sake of learning and furthering their goal. The nature of the coaching typically reveals new perspectives that allow the client to break through blocks in their thinking and to have revelations and transformation.

What Is the Average Time Clients Meet with a Coach?

The length of a coaching engagement differs depending on the coaching client's need or agenda. For example, a coaching engagement can be structured to last six months. In some instances, the coaching client may find it beneficial to work with a coach for a shorter or longer period. According to the ICF, factors that may influence the length of time include the types of goals, the ways individuals or teams prefer to work, the frequency of coaching meetings and financial resources available to support coaching.

Guidelines for Coaches

This section provides details about requirements, policies, and procedures for Coaches. [Adapt for the needs of your organization]

Overview of Requirements

Generally, Coaches-in-Training and Certified Coaches are required to do the following:

- Coach 24 hours per year, starting the fiscal year after their initial certification
- Attend a minimum of three Community of Practice learning events (and/or other approved coach-related learning events) per year.
- Log their learning in the online record system in SharePoint
- Use the Coaching Agreement form with every client
- Send a link to the online Coach Feedback form to every client at the conclusion of the Coaching Engagement
- Maintain their Coaching Hours in an online database
- Adhere to Ethical Standards—ICF and the Coaching Code of Ethics

Logging Hours for Coaching and Learning

There is an online SharePoint site [adapt to your own location and requirements] called the *Coaches Community of Practice* for all CITs and Certified Coaches that coaches can access to log your hours and find resources.

1. Coaches should complete their Coaching Log on the ICF Coaching Log excel spreadsheet. (Download the template here: https://coachfederation.org/experience-requirements.) Ensure that each client occupies only one line, that a date range is provided and a total number of coaching hours is listed. The final date is simply the last time the coach met with the client.
2. Follow the direction on Client log page to upload the hours into the SharePoint site. Those challenged by this process can reach out to the coaching team at [your email address].
3. Coaches will continue to maintain their hours on the SharePoint from this point on.

Professional Development through Community of Practice

All coaches are required to attend three learning events each year and are required to log that learning on the Client log page.

In-person and virtual learning events are announced in an email coming from the Coaching Program Office. The title of the email is usually "updates from the Coaching Program." When possible, the events are offered twice in the same day to accommodate multiple locations around the globe.

Other Options for Learning

Coaches may seek options for learning about coaching from other venues. They may join an ICF learning event, watch YouTube demonstrations and read books about coaching. Any learning they do can count for the learning requirement provided a similar procedure is applied as above and the learning is documented in the learning log.

The Coaching Agreement

[Your agency name] has a Coaching Agreement form that all Coaches must use with their clients. This Coaching Agreement was approved by the Office of General Council and may not be adapted if used within [your agency name]. Clients must sign the Coaching Agreement before the start of the second session with the client. When delivering the Coaching Agreement, the Coach reviews the agreement in detail with the client.

The coaching agreement between the coach and coaching client is a very important part of the coaching process. Having a written agreement establishes a clear understanding between the coaching client and the coach about the parameters of the coaching relationship, including logistics and scheduling.

In forming coaching agreements around confidentiality, coaches should be aware and inform their clients of the limits of confidentiality by law as it relates to federal employees.

Limits of confidentiality include a report of an act of fraud, waste, or abuse; the revelation of having committed a crime; the threat of harm to self or others; the sharing of information in violation of a security clearance; the report of sexual harassment; the requirement by law or a court order to share particular information. Note: Government policies that refer to conduct in the workplace supersede the general rules of the ICF.

Distinction between Coaching, Mentoring, Counseling, and Therapy

Making the comparison between Coaching, Mentoring, Counseling, Consulting, and Therapy is an important part of the Coaching Agreement.

Mentoring, in particular, has a strong place in the support and development of employees, but differs from coaching significantly. A mentor is defined as *an experienced and trusted advisor*. A mentor is typically more experienced than the person being mentored. A coach does not need to be an expert in the client's formal occupational role and may have never held a job at the coaching client's level. A mentor can be informal or formal and is not required to receive a certification or training to share their experience. Coaches in the coaching program must complete training through a formal coaching training program. Unlike the mentor who provides advice, the coach is an inquirer of the coaching client's thoughts, intentions, desires, and goals.

Counseling/Therapy is another service practice (provided through the Employee Assistance Program in the Office of Human Resources) that is always conducted by professional counselors and psychologists who have received specific training that focuses on clinical diagnoses and therapy of patients. When compared to therapy or counseling, while positive feelings and emotions may be a natural outcome of coaching, the primary focus is on creating actionable strategies for achieving specific goals in one's work or personal life. The emphasis in a coaching relationship is on setting and attaining goals through future action, accountability, and follow through, while the emphasis in counseling or therapy focuses on reflecting on past circumstances, emotions, and behaviors.

See the table below for further distinctions.

Mentoring	Coaching	Counseling/Therapy
Ongoing relationship that can last for a long period of time.	Relationship generally has a set duration, typically about six months. Coaching focuses on "how" to develop behaviors to support the client's future.	Most counseling helps the client to understand *why* behaviors developed.
Can be more informal and meetings can take place as and when the mentee needs some advice, guidance, or support.	Generally, more structured in nature and meetings are scheduled on a regular basis. The goal is to improve an individual's development and performance.	Goal is to help people understand the root causes of longstanding performance problems/issues at work.

Mentoring	Coaching	Counseling/Therapy
Mentor is usually more experienced and qualified than the "mentee." Often a senior person in the organization who can pass on knowledge, experience, and open doors to otherwise out-of-reach opportunities. A key distinction from coaching is that the mentor has a stake in the outcome.	Coaching is generally not performed on the basis that the coach needs to have direct experience of their client's formal occupational role, unless the coaching is specific and skills-focused. The coach has no stake in the outcome. Coaching does not seek to resolve any underlying psychological problems. It assumes a person does not require a psycho-social intervention.	Counseling can be used to address psycho-social as well as performance issues.
Mentoring revolves around developing the mentee as a professional.	Coaches pay attention to exploring the potential impact of decisions and actions on all areas of life and with a long-term view.	

Behaving Ethically

The coach and the client are first of all two government employees who are bound by a coaching agreement, which is a confidentiality agreement between the two parties. The coach and client are required to keep a copy of the coaching agreement for the time they are in the coaching engagement. At the conclusion of the coaching engagement, the coaching agreement is destroyed.

If an issue comes up during the coaching that the coach needs help with, the coach can reach out to the Coach Program Managers who will review the case and determine the best way to assist the coach or to elevate a concern. Examples of things that a coach may need help with:

- The coach recognizes a conflict of interest in working with the client
- The coach feels they cannot coach on an issue because of personal circumstance cloud their ability to coach
- The coach thinks that the client is behaving unethically

Conflicts of Interest

Internal federal coaches face a risk for potential conflict of interest situations when working as a coach within their own organizations. It is important for internal federal coaches to avoid situations which present a conflict of interest. Such instances include but may not be limited to:

- Engaging in a coaching relationship as an internal coach with a current direct report
- Engaging in a coaching relationship as an internal coach with someone who will imminently become a direct report
- Engaging in a coaching relationship as an internal coach with a current manager in one's supervisory chain
- Engaging in a coaching relationship as an internal coach with a federal employee and receiving payment outside of regular salary compensation

Coach Qualifications, Certifications, and Credentials

Standards for coach training programs are provided by organizations dedicated to defining the standards. There are several organizations in the world that provide guidance for credentialing. [your organization's name] chose to follow the guidelines of the International Coach Federation (ICF), which is one of the largest credentialing agencies in the world to ensure that the program used to train coaches contains the elements needed to consistently develop excellent coaches. Once completing the Certification Program and receiving the certification, the coach can choose to pursue other credentials, such as the one offered through the ICF.

Credentialing in coaching is based on two factors, the learning of coaching skills and the minimum qualifications for coaching.

- Qualified Coach—Means that the coach has the qualifications to coach. Qualifications are usually certificates, given at the completion of a training program, or credentials, awarded by a professional accrediting body, such as the International Coach Federation.
- Certified Coach—A Certified Coach is someone who has earned a certificate from a credentialing body-approved coaching program, one that teaches coach competencies and ethics and provides individual mentoring and opportunities for coach practice.

- Credentialed Coach—A credential is earned from a professional organization that sets the standards for the profession. The first credential that ICF offers for coaches is Associate Certified Coach (ACC). Earning a credential is achieved by applying through ICF. It does not require a credential to coach at, nor does it pay for the application of a credential. The Coaching Program Office will support coaches seeking their ACC by certifying the coach's hours to the International Coach Federation at the coach's request.
- For the purposes of determining the coach qualifications for the Coaching Program, [your organization name] has established a tiered level of credentials for coaches.

Designation Name	Origin of Qualification	Approved Coaching Activities
Coach-in-Training	This is a coach who has completed three weeks of the in-person coach training provided through the contract training. At this point, they are entered on the official database of coaches and will remain a CIT until the coach completes the requirements to become a Certified Coach.	CITs are approved to conduct internal coaching at. An employee may select them in the CoP database and they may be assigned to a client by the program manager. They are not authorized to coach or be coached by another CIT, but may coach or be coached by a Certified Coach or higher.
Certified Coach (Qualified Coach)	Has received a Certificate of Professional Coaching from an ICF-approved training program and has submitted the certificate to the program manager. Receives the designation of Certified Coach, which is maintained through ongoing learning and coaching requirements.	Can coach any employee and can coach student coaches in the training program for the 6-hour requirement to be coached as a Program Coach.
Senior Certified Coach	Has documented 100 hours or more of coaching experience.	Can coach any employee and can coach student coaches in the training program for the 6-hour requirement to be coached as a Program Coach. May also serve as a Mentor to Coaches and is eligible for Mentor Training.

Designation Name	Origin of Qualification	Approved Coaching Activities
Credentialed Coach (ACC, PCC, other)	Has earned a credential from an accrediting professional organization, such as ICF.	Can coach any employee and can coach student coaches in the training program for the 6-hour requirement to be coached as a Program Coach. Can also serve as a Mentor Coach to Coaches and is eligible for Mentor Training.

Re-Certification Requirements

After the coach has received their initial certificates as described in the previous section, the Certified Coach status remains active for three fiscal years, starting the next fiscal year following their certification. The Coaching Program office will initiate a review at that time and will look for evidence and documentation of the following:

- Coaching for 24 hours every year, or 72 hours over the three years. These hours will be recorded in the Coaching Community of Practice Coaches Log
- Attend a minimum of three Coaching-related learning events per year. These events are also recorded by the participant in their Learning log (located in the same place as the Coaches log)
- Should the Certified Coach designation lapse, the coach's status will be changed to inactive. The Coach may request to be changed to active status again, should they want to pursue coaching more actively again.

Additional Information for Coaches

The Coach's Role

The coach's role is to support the client's professional development by asking powerful questions, assigning developmental tasks, and challenging the client to stretch to reach greater heights. The Coach:

- Provides objective assessment and observations that foster self-awareness and awareness of others.
- Listens closely to fully understand the circumstances.

- Serves as a sounding board to explore possibilities and implement thoughtful planning and decision making.
- Champions opportunities and potential, encouraging the client to reach out and challenge situations commensurate with strengths and aspirations.
- Fosters shifts in thinking that reveal fresh perspectives.
- Challenges blind spots to illuminate new possibilities and support creation of alternative scenarios.
- Maintains professional boundaries in the coaching relationship, including confidentiality, and the adherence to the coaching profession's code of ethics.

The Client's Role

A client is ready for coaching when they are willing to devote the time and energy to make real changes in their actions and behaviors. The Client:

- Determines their own coaching goals, topics, and agenda.
- Is willing to explore possibilities, new ideas, and fresh perspectives.
- Takes courageous action in alignment with personal goals and aspirations.
- Engages in big-picture thinking.
- Utilizes the tools, concepts, models, and principles provided by the coach.
- Assumes full responsibility for personal decisions and actions.
- Is accountable to the coach and respects the coach's time and completes assigned tasks.

Leader as Coach

A per the [your agency policy] and as per the ICF code of ethics, a coach is not allowed to have an official coaching relationship with anyone in their chain of command. A leader is allowed to engage in coach-like conversations with their direct reports and can have any learning-related counseling conversations consistent with civilian personnel policies, including Individual Development Plans and Career Development Plans. It is recommended that they do not coach anyone for whom they have any influence in terms of feedback for appraisals or promotions. In summary, a leader who is a trained coach may coach anyone outside their chain of command and may use coach-like skills with those within their chain of command.

Supervisors of Coaching Clients

Supervisor in this context is the rater of record of the client.

- Grants permission for coaching: Employees are authorized to receive coaching during duty hours with the permission of their supervisors and as mission permits.
- Supervisors of Coaches
- Supervisor in this context is the rater of record of the student.
- Grants permission for employees to become coaches: Employees are authorized to receive Coach Training with the permission of their supervisor. The supervisor also attests to the coach applicant's eligibility to attend the program through the application process.
- Grants permission for Coaches to coach during duty hours: A supervisor may limit the hours that a coach is allowed to coach during duty hours based on mission requirements. Supervisors should take under consideration that they approved the coach's participation for a minimum of 24 coaching hours and a minimum of three coaching-related learning events per year.

Coach Mentors

Coach Mentors are Certified Coaches who have received additional training that allows them to provide specific feedback to Certified Coaches on their coaching competencies. Coaches can request mentoring directly from the list of coach mentors below. The mentor–coach relationship is similar to the mentor–coach relationship experienced during your coach training program and is ultimately up to the mentor and coach. Examples of activities include providing a recording and transcript of the coaching to the mentor coach who listens to the recording and provides detailed written and verbal feedback to the coach. The mentor will point out evidence of demonstrated competencies and will provide recommendations for coaching responses and questions differently.

Coaching Supervisors

Coaching Supervision is a collaborative learning practice to continually build the capacity of the coach through reflective dialogue for the benefit of both coaches and clients. It focuses on the development of the coach's capacity through offering a richer and broader opportunity for support and development. Coaching Supervision creates a safe environment for the coach to share their successes and failures in becoming masterful in the way they work with their clients.

Coaching Program Manager (PM)

Program Managers manage the Coaching Program and are responsible for making training opportunities available to the civilian workforce through the Coaches Community of Practice. Program managers establish administrative controls, maintain infrastructure, and provide services to support Coaching program; promulgate policy, procedures, and business rules required for effective administration of Coaching programs; maintain a current annual catalog of the Coaching program; identify new opportunities and recommend additions and/or deletions of the Coaching program; determine number of applications allowed for the Coaching program and required training; maintain official records pertaining to personnel participation and submit to their leadership annually as required; provide announcements of the Coaching program to personnel; and screen applications for eligibility and completeness.

The PMs' roles include maintaining official records pertaining to personnel participation in Coaching program and responding to requests for information concerning these records; including the collection of program completion documentation.

Sample Frequently Asked Questions

What Is Coaching?

The International Coach Federation defines coaching as partnering with clients in a thought-provoking and creative process that inspires them to maximize their personal and professional potential, which is particularly important in today's uncertain and complex environment. Being coached is an excellent way to achieve professional and career goals, solve individual leadership challenges, and excel in self-awareness and self-management.

Through structured dialogue, coaches assist their clients to see new perspectives and achieve greater clarity about their own thoughts, emotions, and actions, and about the people and situations around them. The client gives power to the relationship, drives the coaching agenda, and is ultimately responsible for the outcome of the coaching engagement. Coaches apply specific techniques and skills, approaches, and methodologies that enable the clients to develop their goals and design actions to achieve them.

Coaching is one of the most valuable developmental resources and has been linked to positive outcomes such as increased productivity, retention, and engagement. A successful coaching engagement promotes and sustains professional growth and competence.

Who Should Work with a Coach?

Everyone needs a coach at some time. Anyone who wants to partner with a professional to examine any aspect of their life and consider perspectives and options to create a path forward should consider a coach. Coaching can help you work through a challenge or take advantage of an opportunity. Coaching topics and goals in the federal government setting should be aligned with the employee's professional goals and organizational mission.

What Happens During a Coaching Session?

The client shares their topic and, along with the coach, identifies a specific outcome for the session. The coach listens and asks questions designed to assist the client to take perspectives, explore options, identify actions, and be accountable.

What Is the Coach's Role?

The Coach:

- Provides objective assessment and observations that foster self-awareness and awareness of others.
- Listens closely to fully understand the circumstances.
- Serves as a sounding board to explore possibilities and implement thoughtful planning and decision making.
- Champions opportunities and potential, encouraging the client to reach out and challenge situations commensurate with strengths and aspirations.
- Fosters shifts in thinking that reveal fresh perspectives.
- Challenges blind spots to illuminate new possibilities and support creation of alternative scenarios.
- Maintains professional boundaries in the coaching relationship, including confidentiality, and the adherence to the coaching profession's code of ethics.

What Is the Client's Role?

The client must be willing to devote the time and energy to make real changes in their actions and behaviors. The best clients are ready to work and be fully engaged in the process. They are committed to their growth and are ready to act. The client should always come prepared for their session by having a focus for the discussion. They are open to change, able to put their plans and learning into action. In addition, they are honest, able to explore uncomfortable areas, and respectful during the process.

The Client:

- Determines their own coaching goals, topics, and agenda.
- Is willing to explore possibilities, new ideas, and fresh perspectives.
- Takes courageous action in alignment with personal goals and aspirations.
- Engages in big-picture thinking.
- Utilizes the tools, concepts, models, and principles provided by the coach.

How Often and How Long Are Coaching Sessions?

The coach and client will agree on how often to meet and the length of the sessions during their intake session. Generally, sessions are from 45 to 60 minutes.

What If I Do Not Like My Coach?

Sometimes, matches do not work. If at any time you do not feel comfortable with your coach, reach out to the program manager to discuss the situation and options.

How Is Coaching Different from Mentoring?

Mentors have experience or expertise they are willing to share in an area the mentee is pursuing. They provide guidance, advice, feedback, encouragement, and inspiration to their mentee. A coach does not need to be an expert in one area because they do not direct the client but assists them in discovering their own path. Like mentoring, coaching is considered a developmental activity, which enables individuals to achieve their full potential. While a mentor provides advice, guidance, and subject-matter expertise, a coach uses a process to mutually define actions for professional development without the coach providing any advice. Furthermore, formal coaching is always predicated on a signed agreement between coach and client, sating the ethical standards of confidentiality, voluntariness, and self-determination, including the duration of the coaching agreement and the expectations of both parties. It is important to understand the distinctions between these roles to ensure the appropriate use in the workplace.

How Is Coaching Different from Consulting?

Consultants are experts who are paid to solve problems. They diagnose and then propose a solution. They often will implement the solution. Coaches ask questions so the client can identify and create an implementation plan for solutions. This allows clients to develop their own way forward and build problem-solving capabilities.

How Is Coaching Different from Counseling?

Counselors work to identify issues from clients' past that are preventing them from moving forward successfully. They work to bring healing and closure to past issues so clients can move forward. Coaches may use similar exploratory and communication techniques; coaching starts in the present and is future oriented.

Where Will Coaching Occur?

Most coaching occurs virtually, either by phone or communication software, although some coaches meet in person. The client and coach decide what will work for them. Typically, coaches meet with clients for one-hour sessions every two to three weeks while working toward their desired goal.

Who Can Perform Coaching in the Federal Government?

Coaching can be performed by certified internal or external coach and by leaders who have received training in coaching skills. The certification is provided by the training institution that provided the formal training. Coaches who have formal training are not required to have additional coaching credentials to be qualified to coach in the federal government.

How Does Formal Coaching Work?

Employees can work with a Federal government Internal Coach or an External Coach that is provided by their agency. The relationship is established with a coaching agreement that describes the roles and responsibilities of the coach and the client. There are no requirements for the length of a coaching meeting, the number of meetings, or the duration of the engagement. It is recommended that the coach and client work to establish the overall goal for the engagement and establish a goal for each coaching meeting.

What Is the Difference Between an Internal Coach and an External Coach?

An *Internal Coach* is a certified professional coach who is employed within the federal government and provides coaching services to other federal employees in addition to their regular duties. An *External Coach* is a certified professional coach, who is either self-employed or partners with other professional coaches to form a coaching business.

What Is Informal Coaching?

A supervisor, manager, or executive who leverages coaching knowledge, approaches, and techniques in working with his or her employees to build awareness and support positive behavior is using *informal* coaching versus the *formal* coaching. These leaders, whether they are certified coaches or not, cannot have an official coaching relationship with their direct reports because this would be a conflict of interest. Formal coaching is done by a certified professional internal or external coach who has certifications and/or credentials.

What Are Some Common Issues Tackled During a Coaching Engagement?

Individuals may engage in coaching for a variety of reasons related to maximizing performance. Examples of potential coaching objectives include the following:

- Develop leadership skills of technical experts interested in supervisory positions
- Facilitate professional transitions (e.g., transition from non-supervisory to supervisory roles, transition into higher-level leadership roles)
- Organize and prioritize professional responsibilities
- Clarify vision, create meaningful goals, and develop achievable action steps
- Facilitate change management
- Achieve professional career goals
- Streamline or identify functional efficiencies
- Solve individual leadership challenges
- Excel in self-awareness and self-management
- Identify core strengths and recognize how best to leverage them
- Gain clarity in purpose and decision making
- Strengthening leadership competencies

Are Coaching Sessions Confidential?

All information discussed during a coaching engagement is confidential unless the client gives explicit permission to share or as required by law. A coaching agreement must include a statement of confidentiality that informs clients of the limits of confidentiality as it relates to federal government employees. Limits of confidentiality in the federal government include a report of an act of fraud, waste, or abuse; the revelation of having committed a crime; the threat of harm to self or others; the sharing of information in violation of a security clearance; the report of sexual harassment; the requirement by law or a court order to share particular information.

What Ethical Standards Are Expected to be Followed for Coaching in the Federal Government?

Federal government internal coaches are bound to uphold the basic obligation for public service and the code of ethics associated with the coaching credentialing organization that approves or accredits the coaching program where they received their coach training.

Can an Internal Coach Act as a Coach to Anyone in the Federal Government?

Federal government internal coaches need to avoid situations where they are coaching individuals who could be in their chain of command. Such instances include:

- Engaging in a coaching relationship as an internal coach with a current direct report
- Engaging in a coaching relationship as an internal coach with someone who will imminently become a direct report
- Engaging in a coaching relationship as an internal coach with a current manager in one's supervisory chain
- Engaging in a coaching relationship as an internal coach with a government employee and receiving payment outside of regular salary compensation

What Record-Keeping Is Required for Coaching Engagements?

Coaching in any capacity is considered professional development if the goal of the engagement relates to an organization-related outcome. As with any other authorized development activity, time spent in professional coaching, either as an internal federal coach or client, must be approved by the employee's supervisor with consideration for organizational priorities. Agencies should develop a method for documenting coaching hours as part of their program.

Sample Request to Join Coach Cadre

If you have already completed coach training or are a certified coach, we would like to invite you to become a member of our Coach Cadre. The benefits to being a member of the Coach Cadre include:

- Receiving clients to coach without marketing.
- Attending training on a regular basis from certified coaches and guest presenters.
- Networking with other coaches and those interested in coaching.

To become a member of the Coach Cadre, you must provide verification of your training or certification and meet with one of our coaches to learn about our program. Please send a copy of your coach training certificates or proof of certification along with the information below to: Program Email.

Name	
Organization	
Job Title	
E-mail Address	
Coach Training Completed Name of Course and Number of Hours	
Attached Training/ICF Certification Documentation	

If you have any other questions or need further information, please contact us at Program Email.

Sample Coach Bio

Insert Your Picture Here

Name

Address
Timezone
Phone
Email

Education

Coach Training Program, 2022
Degree,
University, 1990

Credentials

Coaching and others

Functional Experience

- Using bullets, provide functional areas you have worked in

Coaching Philosophy

Share a description of your coach approach and style. You may want to include instruments you use frequently. Also, please insert a picture here.

Coaching Specialization

Share your coaching niche(s), for example, Professional and Personal Visioning; Transitions and Paradigm Shifts.

Career Highlights

Provide a brief description of your career in paragraph or bullet form. Be sure to include where you have worked and major accomplishments

Other Information

Please provide any other information you would like to share! This can be personal or professional—you choose.

Sample Coach Development Plan

Coaches are always learning and being intentional about your development is important. If you are credentialed through ICF, you need to obtain Continuing Coach Educations Units (CCEUs) to renew your certification. Review the ICF site to obtain the latest guidance for your credential.

Name	Email/Telephone Number
Overall Development Goal/Outcome	

Select Areas for Improvement:	
☐ **ICF Core Competency: A. Foundation** (1. Demonstrates Ethical Practice; 2. Embodies a Coaching Mindset) ☐ **ICF Core Competency: B. Co-Creating the Relationship** (3. Establishes and Maintains Agreement; 4. Cultivates Trust and Safety; 5. Maintains Presence) ☐ **ICF Core Competency: C. Communicating Effectively** (6. Listens Actively; 7. Evokes Awareness) ☐ **ICF Core Competency: D. Cultivating Learning and Growth** (8. Facilitates Client Growth; Creating Awareness; Designing Actions; Planning and Goal Setting; Managing Progress and Accountability) ☐ **ICF Resource Development** (Training, writing, research, or self-study outside of the ICF Core Competencies that contributes to the professional development of a coach.)	☐ **Leading Change-ECQ 1** (creativity and innovation, external awareness, flexibility, resilience, strategic thinking, vision) ☐ **Leading People-ECQ 2** (conflict management, leveraging diversity, developing others, team building) ☐ **Results Driven-ECQ 3** (accountability, customer service, decisiveness, entrepreneurship, problem solving, technical credibility) ☐ **Business Acumen-ECQ 4** (financial management, human capital management, technology management) ☐ **Building Coalitions-ECQ 5** (partnering, political savvy, influencing/negotiating) ☐ **Fundamental Competencies** (interpersonal skills, oral communication, integrity/honesty, written communication, continual learning, public service motivation) ☐ **Other:**

ICF Competency or ECQ (1–5)	Developmental Activity	Learning Goal	Targeted Timeframe for Completion	Completion Date & CCEUs

Sample Coach Request

Application must be completed by applicant and submitted to _Program Email_.

Name:					
Email Address:					
Phone Number:					
Organization:					
Job Title:					
Grade/Level:		Preferred Pronouns:		Time Zone:	
Preferred Meeting Time (check all that apply)	☐ Morning	☐ Midday		☐ Afternoon	

The International Coach Federation defines coaching as partnering with clients in a thought-provoking and creative process that inspires them to maximize their personal and professional potential, which is particularly important in today's uncertain and complex environment.

How is coaching distinct from other development or support options? Professional coaching focuses on setting goals, creating outcomes, and managing personal change. The emphases in a coaching relationship are on action, accountability, and follow through. Coaches do not offer advice or decide on the topics to discuss. They respect the client's decisions and keep all discussions confidential. If you are searching for someone to provide guidance and advice, you should explore working with a mentor.

Being coached is an excellent way to achieve professional and career goals, solve individual leadership challenges, and excel in self-awareness and self-management. To assist in assigning a coach, please complete the following questions.

1. List two goals or outcomes you would like to achieve through coaching.
2. Provide a one- to two-paragraph bio
3. Additional Information that may be helpful in assigning a coach
4. If you would like a specific coach, please provide the coach's name.

For additional information or if you have questions, contact us at _Program Email_.

Sample Intake Session Outline

During the intake session, the coach develops an understanding of the client's needs and way of working, and it helps the client understand what coaching is, what to expect, and the role of the coach and client.

What Are the Client's Expectations?

- What are your expectations?
- What goals do you have?
- How will you know when you have achieved those goals?
- What are your reasons for seeking coaching now?

What Is Coaching?

- What do you know about coaching?
- Have you had a coach before? If so, what worked well for you? What did the coach do that helped you reach your goals?
- What do you want to know about the coaching process?

Review Agreements and Assumptions (Be Sure to Have the Agreement Signed)

- Discuss Confidentiality.
- Determine frequency and length of sessions.
- Coaching works best when we honor times and dates—define the cancellation policies.
- It is important that we provide immediate feedback on what's working and what is not working in our relationship.
- It's the client's agenda, I suggest client keep a list and come with client session topic.
- Sessions involve lots of questions and reflections—sometimes we use tools or models (provide examples you use).
- May I have permission to…

  - Share if I believe I see patterns
  - Hold you accountable for action AND learning
  - Provide reflection questions/exercises for in between sessions
  - Interrupt/Bottom line—I don't need all the details and we only have an hour each session

- After you've addressed a topic and accomplished something we typically: (a) acknowledge and celebrate; (b) terminate the relationship; or (c) repeat the cycle with other topics of your dream.

Review Client and Coach Roles

- As the client
  - Provide the agenda or topic for each session
  - Come to sessions ready to be honest and open
  - Be willing to experiment and embrace change
  - Be accountable for your commitments and actions

- As the coach I
  - Hold the space for our explorations
  - Assist to clarify and maintain focus on your goals
  - Work with you to consider different perspectives
  - Challenge you and raise your self-awareness
  - Assist you to identify learning
  - Work with you to identify options and develop strategies
  - Help you define accountability for what you say you're going to do
  - Encourage and support you on your journey

What Do You Want to Know About Me?

Getting to know the Client: (Select questions to ask)

- What would you like to share with me?
- What energizes you? When do you feel happiest?
- What makes you feel most fulfilled?
- What are your two top strengths?
- What are your most important values?
- What are your biggest challenges or obstacles?
- What areas of your life would you like to improve?
- What's hard for you to address/admit? What are you avoiding?
- How do you like to develop professionally?
- How do you like to receive feedback?

What Would Be Most Helpful from Your Coach?

- What else is important for me to know about you and your situation?

Sample Coaching Agreement

DIA Coaching Agreement
DIA Certified Coaches and Coaches-in-Training conduct coaching activities as a collateral duty, during regular business hours, with the permission of their supervisors. This agreement is used in conjunction with the Academy of Defense Intelligence (ADI) Administrative Instruction XXX. The Coach and Client or Coachee are required to keep a copy of the agreement for the duration of the coaching engagement and may discard the document and the conclusion of the engagement.

Coach Information

Name:	
Phone:	
Email:	

Client/Coachee Information

Name:	
Phone:	
Email:	

Overview of Coaching Relationship and Terms of Agreement
Client should review, adjust, sign where indicated, and return one copy to Coach at the first session.

Client will receive coaching through the term of this agreement. The initial term of the coaching agreement will be for____sessions beginning on_____and ending on_____. Client or coach can agree to end the agreement at any time. At any time, if the coach or client feels that the coaching relationship is not a good fit, either can request reassignment by contacting the Academy for Defense Intelligence (ADI) Coaching Program Managers at (XXX) XXX-XXXX or coaching.program@ xxxxx.xxx or by selecting their own new coach via the DIA Community of Practice Website. Client and Coach may initiate a new Coaching Agreement upon the conclusion of this agreement if an additional coaching period is requested.

Coaching Assumptions
The Coach is trained in the coaching process, which utilizes an agenda and open-ended questions to allow the Client to reach his or her own answers. The Coaching relationship is based on the premise that the Client is naturally creative and resourceful and knows the best "next" steps and solutions for themselves and that the Client is open to candid self-assessment and is interested in personal development and learning.

Coaching includes value clarification, brainstorming ideas, identifying plans of action, examining modes of operating in life, asking clarifying questions, and making empowering requests.

Coaching includes increasing a Client's effectiveness professionally and personally. Coaching may address specific personal projects, business successes, or general conditions in the Client's life or profession in support of the Client's productivity and development in the workplace.

Coaching is not the same as mentoring. The Coach will not provide guidance or advice based on prior life or work experience.

Coaching is not psychotherapy, psychological counseling, or any type of therapy.

Coaching is not used for any type of professional, legal, medical, financial, or business advice.

Understandings

Appointments

The number of coaching sessions is determined by the Coach and Client after an initial intake session where goals for coaching are determined. Coaching sessions will occur every one to four weeks or as agreed by the Coach and the Client.

The Coach is available Monday through Friday as their schedule permits. Coaching is conducted during regularly scheduled working hours with the permission of the Coach's supervisor and Coachee's supervisor.

The Coach can accept meeting requests through Outlook email and/or phone call. If a client needs a same-day phone session to discuss a specific issue, the Client should email the Coach and suggest a few available times. If the Coach can accommodate a same-day request, the Coach will respond via calendar invite and/or reply email.

Coaching sessions may take place either in person at a mutually agreed upon location or via the telephone or other communication technology. The Client and Coach will do their best to secure privacy and eliminate distractions to promote confidentiality and comfort for the client.

Coaching is scheduled at the mutual convenience of the Coach and the Client. The day and time for the next meeting will be scheduled before the close of each Coaching session.

The Coach and Client are responsible for rescheduling conflicts 24 hours in advance.

Responsibility for Actions

The Client understands that decisions for how to handle issues and to implement choices is exclusively the Client's responsibility.

The Client assumes the responsibility as a DIA Officer to find out about all DIA services and resources available to them.

In the event that the Client feels the need for professional counseling or therapy, it is the responsibility of the Client to seek a licensed professional. Coaching is not to be used in lieu of professional advice. The Client will seek professional guidance for legal, medical, financial, business, or other matters. The Client understands that all decisions in these areas are exclusively his/hers and acknowledges that decisions and actions are his/her responsibility.

The Coach will engage in formal coaching relationships with DIA employees outside of their current chain of command.

Responsibility for Success

The Client agrees to make coaching a priority. Throughout the working relationship, the Coach will engage in direct and personal conversation. The Client can count on the Coach to be honest and straightforward in asking questions and making requests.

The Coach and Client are both 100% responsible for ensuring the Client is receiving the best possible coaching. If either party thinks that is not happening, that party will surface it as a topic for discussion and action. If the Client is unsatisfied with that discussion, he or she should contact the ADI Coaching Program Managers at XXX-XXX-XXXX.

If either Coach or Client decides there is not a good fit, the client or coach can agree to end the agreement at any time. The Client can request reassignment by contacting the Academy for Defense Intelligence (ADI) Coaching Program Managers at (XXX) XXX-XXXX or coaching.program@ xxxxx.xxx or by selecting their own new coach via the DIA Community of Practice Website.

Confidentiality

The Client understands that information between the Coach and Client will be held as confidential by the Coach unless expressly stated otherwise, or disclosure is required by law, regulation, to assist with an investigation, litigation, or for official purposes.

The Coach will adhere to the federal, Department of Defense, and DIA principles of ethical conduct, including the DIA Coaching Code of Ethics in all interactions (see ADI AI006).

The Coach will take the appropriate action with DIA authorities, or ADI, to address any ethics violation or possible breach as soon as the coach becomes aware, whether it involves the Client or others. The Coach will report knowledge of any professional or personal misconduct to the appropriate DIA authorities.

The Client understands that certain topics may be anonymously shared with other coaching professionals for training, consultation, or illustrative purposes.

The Client understands that their name, organization, contact info, dates of the coaching relationship, and number of hours coached will be reported to the ADI Coaching Program Coordinator for data compilation purposes. Aggregate information on the Coaching program will be shared with Department and Agency leaders but no personal information will be shared unless required to do so.

The Client understands that their name, organization, contact information, dates of the coaching *relationship, and number of hours coached will be used as part of the professional Client log required* for various levels of credentialing to external bodies. A Client may request to have their name replaced with a generic placeholder name on any coaching logs that are submitted to an external body. The DIA Coaching Program Manager assumes the responsibility of verifying coaching hours on behalf of the submitting Coach.

Coach will ensure the privacy of Client appointments to include others with access to his/her calendar or knowledge of Coach's appointments, such as Executive Assistant

The Client understands that their name, organization, contact info, dates of the coaching relationship, and number of hours coached will be reported to the ADI Coaching Program Coordinator for data compilation purposes. Aggregate information on the Coaching program will be shared with Department and Agency leaders but no personal information will be shared unless required to do so.

The Client understands that their name, organization, contact information, dates of the coaching *relationship, and number of hours coached will be used as part of the professional Client log required* for various levels of credentialing to external bodies. A Client may request to have their name replaced with a generic placeholder name on any coaching logs that are submitted to an external body. The DIA Coaching Program Manager assumes the responsibility of verifying coaching hours on behalf of the submitting Coach.

Coach will ensure the privacy of Client appointments to include others with access to his/her calendar or knowledge of Coach's appointments, such as Executive Assistants.

Coach's Credentials

The DIA Coach has completed training in a Coach Federation (ICF) accredited coaching program, is working on accumulating hours, and/or is a DIA Certified Coach. Coaching Credentials can be verified through the DIA Coaching Program Manager. (XXX) XXX-XXXX or coaching.program@ xxxxx.xxx

Agreement
The signatures on this agreement indicate full understanding of/and agreement with the information outlined above.

Client Signature:	Date:
Coach Signature:	Date:

Sample Assignment Emails

Sample Assignment Email from Program Manager

Thank you for choosing coaching. You have been assigned a coach who is copied on this email. Your coach will be in contact with you within five business days. If you have any questions regarding this coaching assignment, please contact **Program Manager Name**, at: *Program Email.*

Your coaching services will be **INSERT TIME PERIOD or NUMBER OF SESSIONS** upon receipt of this email. During the next week, your coach will reach out to you and you should set up a time to have an initial meeting to get started.

After the first meeting, you and the coach will sign a coaching agreement which includes such items as individual responsibilities, cancellation times, and preferred contact information. During the coaching, you will come with items to discuss. The coaching assignment can be concluded at any time the client and coach agree.

If you have any questions or feel the coach is not a good match, please contact *Program Email.*

Sample Email for Assigned Coach to Send Once They Have Scheduled Meeting

I look forward to our partnership and working with you toward your goals.

We will conduct our initial meeting on **INSERT DATE AND TIME.**

I have attached the coaching agreement for your review. I can answer any questions and we can adjust it to meet our needs during the initial meeting.

To get the most from your coaching experience, consider the following recommendations.

- Come prepared. It's your agenda—talk about what really matters to you.
- Expect an opportunity to discover your own answers. Coaching utilizes a process involving open-ended questions to allow you to reach your own answers.
- Be open-minded. You will get more out of the experience if you are willing to examine your assumptions, ways of thinking, expectations, beliefs, and reactions.

- Set realistic goals. Coaching should lead to action. Make sure you know what your goals are (I can help you clarify these.)
- Do the work. Reflect and act on agreements you make.
- Get real. Maybe you have never shared your ideas, visions, or emotions before. Don't hold back. Awareness is the first step toward change.
- Be willing to evolve. Coaching is a developmental process; be open to change.
- Be patient. Nothing happens overnight, trust the process.

If you have questions before we meet, please feel free to email or contact me at **xxx-xxx-xxxx**. I look forward to our sessions and am excited about the possibilities of joining you on your journey to meet your goals.

Sample Assignment Check-In

It has been several weeks since you completed your initial coaching agreement, and we want to know how it is going. Thank you in advance for taking just a few minutes to share your thoughts. This information will allow us to train our coaches and improve our processes to serve you and others more effectively.

Use 1 to 5 to rate the following statements based on your sessions using the following rating system:

1. Strongly Disagree 2. Disagree 3. Neutral 4. Agree 5. Strongly Agree

   A. My coach and I established clear goals for our conversations.
   B. My coach listened well, and I felt heard.
   C. My coach communicated clearly.
   D. My coach asked great questions.
   E. I learned more about myself and how I should move forward.
   F. I discovered new and considered options.

Please feel free to add any additional comments. You should not add any specific information about your client.

Sample Coach Reflection Form

Reflecting on your coaching is key to improving your skills. You can use this at the end of a session or an assignment.

1. Use 1 to 5 to rate the following statements using the following rating system:

   1. Never   2. Sometimes   3. Often   4. Regularly   5. Always

   A.   I worked to establish our coaching agreement.
   B.   I worked to establish trust in our sessions.
   C.   I listened well.
   D.   I communicated clearly and directly.
   E.   I asked powerful questions.
   F.   I helped the client expand their awareness and consider different options.
   G.   I used metaphors and models to assist the process.

2.   I prepared for the session(s) by

3.   I am pleased that I

4.   One thing I could do differently is

5.   I have learned

6.   Additional Insights

Sample Coaching Evaluation Questions

1. Use 1 to 5 to rate the following statements based on your sessions using the following rating system:

   1. Strongly Disagree   2. Disagree   3. Neutral   4. Agree   5. Strongly Agree

   A. My coach and I established clear goals for our conversations.
   B. My coach listened well, and I felt heard.
   C. My coach communicated clearly.
   D. My coach asked great questions.
   E. I learned more about myself and how I should move forward.
   F. I discovered new and considered options.

2. What is different because of your coaching experience?
3. I appreciate that my coach
4. One thing my coach could do differently is
5. Additional Comments
6. I would recommend coaching to my colleagues.   ☐ Yes   ☐ No
   Coach's Name (optional):

Sample End of Coaching Engagement Survey

To date, how many meetings have you had with your coach? *

- O   1–2 meetings
- O   3–5 meetings
- O   6–8 meetings
- O   9 or more meetings

Who is your coach? (Select from dropdown) *

[▼]

I am satisfied with the coaching I received *

- O   Strongly Agree
- O   Agree
- O   Disagree
- O   Strongly Disagree

My coach and I had an excellent rapport *

- O   Strongly Agree
- O   Agree
- O   Disagree
- O   Strongly Disagree

My coach was effective in assisting me to identify my development goals and objectives *

- O   Strongly Agree
- O   Agree
- O   Disagree
- O   Strongly Disagree

My coach helped me learn more about myself *

- O   Strongly Agree
- O   Agree
- O   Disagree
- O   Strongly Disagree

My coach helped me learn more about how I relate to others *

- O   Strongly Agree
- O   Agree

O   Disagree
O   Strongly Disagree

Coaching was a transformational experience *

O   Strongly Agree
O   Agree
O   Disagree
O   Strongly Disagree

I feel that I have more skills for success as a result of coaching *

O   Strongly Agree
O   Agree
O   Disagree
O   Strongly Disagree

If you were to sum up your coaching experience in 1–2 sentences, how would you describe it? *

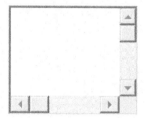

What were the strengths of your coach? *

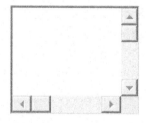

Where can your coach improve? *

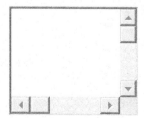

May the coaching program use your feedback for testimonials? Y/N *

Feel free to provide additional comments to improve the overall DIA Coaching Program

Sample Impact Survey I

Directions to Participants: The purpose of this survey is to gather information about how becoming a coach at DIA has affected you and your relationships with your work colleagues. This is separate from your relationships with coaching clients.

The purpose of the following questions is to learn how you perceive your relationships in the workplace have or have not changed as a result of your coaching training.

Directions: Please answer the following questions.

To what extent have your coaching skills improved your relationship with your Direct Reports *

- O   Not at all
- O   A Little
- O   To Some Extent
- O   To a Great Extent
- O   I do not have direct reports

1. Please provide examples

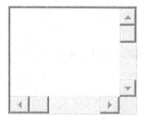

To what extent have your coaching skills affected your leadership performance? *

- O   Not at all
- O   A Little
- O   To Some Extent
- O   To a Great Extent

2.   Please provide examples

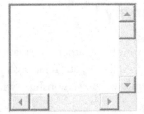

To what extent has learning to be a coach helped you understand the perspective of others? *

- O   Not at all
- O   A Little
- O   To Some Extent
- O   To a Great Extent

3.   Please explain or provide examples

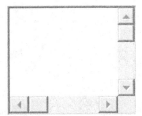

To what extent have your coaching skills improved your relationship with your Supervisors (Team Lead)? *

- O   Not at all
- O   A Little
- O   To Some Extent
- O   To a Great Extent

4.   Please explain or provide examples

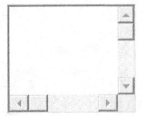

To what extent have your coaching skills improved your relationship with your

Managers? *

○　Not at all
○　A Little
○　To Some Extent
○　To a Great Extent

5.　Please explain or provide examples

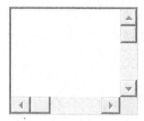

To what extent have your coaching skills improved your relationship to your peers? *

○　Not at all
○　A Little
○　To Some Extent
○　To a Great Extent

6.　Please explain or provide examples

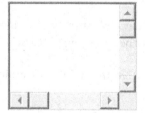

Sample Impact Survey II

Distribute this survey to those in the circle of influence of Internal Coaches.

What is your relationship to the participant who forwarded you this survey?

From your perspective, to what extent did the DIA Officer's coaching skills enhance his or her leadership performance?

O   Not at all
O   A little
O   To Some Extent
O   To a Great Extent

Please explain or provide examples

The following questions ask about coaching behaviors that may have been demonstrated by the DIA Officer before and after becoming a DIA Coach.

1. How often did this DIA Officer ask a question that initiated learning before he/she became a coach? *

   O   Never
   O   Rarely
   O   Frequently
   O   Always
   O   I don't know

2. How often did this DIA Officer focus on his/her complete attention on your conversations and spontaneously build on your relationship before he/she became a coach? *

   O   Never
   O   Rarely

- ⭘ Frequently
- ⭘ Always
- ⭘ I don't know

3. After he / she became a coach? *

- ⭘ Never
- ⭘ Rarely
- ⭘ Frequently
- ⭘ Always
- ⭘ I don't know

4. How often did this DIA Officer make an effort to develop a collaborative and trusting relationship before he / she became a coach? *

- ⭘ Never
- ⭘ Rarely
- ⭘ Frequently
- ⭘ Always
- ⭘ I don't know

5. After he / she became a coach? *

- ⭘ Never
- ⭘ Rarely
- ⭘ Frequently
- ⭘ Always
- ⭘ I don't know

6. How often did this DIA Officer actively listen and reflect on what you were saying or not saying before he / she became a coach? *

- ⭘ Never
- ⭘ Rarely
- ⭘ Frequently
- ⭘ I don't know

7. After he / she became a coach? *

- ⭘ Never
- ⭘ Rarely
- ⭘ Frequently
- ⭘ Always
- ⭘ I don't know

8. How often did this DIA Officer use language that was direct before he/she became a coach? *

   ○ Never
   ○ Rarely
   ○ Frequently
   ○ Always
   ○ I don't know

9. After he/she became a coach? *

   ○ Never
   ○ Rarely
   ○ Frequently
   ○ Always
   ○ I don't know

10. How often did your interactions with this DIA Officer lead to greater awareness, insight, understanding before he/she became a coach? *

   ○ Never
   ○ Rarely
   ○ Frequently
   ○ Always
   ○ I don't know

11. After he/she became a coach? *

   ○ Never
   ○ Rarely
   ○ Frequently
   ○ Always
   ○ I don't know

Only Direct Reports of the DIA Officer should answer the following questions

12. How often did this DIA Coach work with you to design actions that will most effectively promote your growth or job performance before he/she became a coach?

   ○ Never
   ○ Rarely
   ○ Frequently
   ○ Always
   ○ I don't know

13. After he/she became a coach?

   - ○ Never
   - ○ Rarely
   - ○ Frequently
   - ○ Always
   - ○ I don't know

14. How often did this DIA Officer work with you to plan and set goals that will most effectively promote your growth or job performance before he/she became a coach?

   - ○ Never
   - ○ Rarely
   - ○ Frequently
   - ○ Always
   - ○ I don't know

15. After he/she became a coach?

   - ○ Never
   - ○ Rarely
   - ○ Frequently
   - ○ Always
   - ○ I don't know

16. How often did this DIA Officer work with you to hold you accountable for working toward tyour career or job performance goals before he/she became a coach?

   - ○ Never
   - ○ Rarely
   - ○ Frequently
   - ○ Always
   - ○ I don't know

17. After he/she became a coach?

   - ○ Never
   - ○ Rarely
   - ○ Frequently
   - ○ Always
   - ○ I don't know

Appendix 3: Expanding Your Portfolio

Coaching program managers may be in a position where they are looking for alternative ways to instill coaching skills in the workforce. This appendix provides descriptions for several cost-effective ways to make that a reality. In some cases, what we describe here may be all a coaching program can afford to offer to the organization. In other cases, these activities may be add-ons.

Coaching Skills for Everyone

What is the intent of your program? Is it to bring more coach-like skills into the culture? Are you trying to raise awareness, so employees will add coaching skills to their development plans? If you are raising awareness, there are many options to consider. Author talks or book discussions can be effective. Agencies have used *Change your Questions, Change your Life: 10 Powerful Tools for Life and Work* by Marilee Adams in the past. Other books that have been well received include Michael Bungay Stanier's *The Coaching Habit: Say Less, Ask More & Change the Way You Lead Forever* and Alan Fine's *You Already Know How to Be Great: A Simple Way to Remove Interference and Unlock Your Greatest Potential*. You can also provide micro-learning sessions for coaching skills, such as a five-to-ten-minute *Listening Strategies*, at all-hands meetings and use a panel or leaders to share testimonials or stories on the effectiveness of using coaching skills in the workplace.

Are you ready to build skills? Short programs, webinars, and on-demand sessions are effective to introduce concepts and techniques available to employees at all levels. Having a series of Coaching Skills in the Workplace allows you to provide several courses to employees to introduce the basics of creating a coaching mindset, listening well, asking questions, identifying actions, developing a plan, and building self-accountability. Making on-demand coaching skills sessions available on your organization's Learning Management System is also a way to teach skills over time. If you have the resources, you can use the on-demand sessions to provide content and provide practice sessions live or virtually for the participants upon completion.

Creating a short course may democratize coaching in the workplace because it will allow many to attend. A "Coaching Skills for Everyone" course can do that. This can be a short coaching program that provides an opportunity for all employees to understand how to have a coach-like conversation in the workplace. It could cover why coach-like conversations work, provide a model of coaching, teach active listening and the art of asking questions. To be truly effective, it must provide opportunities to practice the coach-like skills with other participants and a plan to transfer the learning to the workplace. The result of a class like this could be employees who are more proactive and better communicators. Training activities are one way to bring coaching skills to an organization and impact the culture in a positive way.

Coaching Skills for Leaders

At DIA, it became widely known that learning to become a coach would enhance a leader's skills as a leader. However, many of them lamented that they didn't have enough time to invest in a 136-hour training course in addition to their very busy day jobs. The DIA Coaching Program Managers observed this gap getting bigger and thought about how they could bring some coaching skills to the leaders who were interested in learning coaching skills but did not have the time or did not desire to take the full coaching course. Using their own experience of being leaders in the agency and their expertise in coaching and instructional design, they developed a course called, "Coaching Skills for Leaders."

Coaching Skills for Leaders is a three-day course that focuses on supervisors and their communications with direct reports in the workplace. The course is held virtually and in person. It opens with a live roleplay conducted between two facilitators. One plays the role of the supervisor and the other plays the role of the employee. The roleplay is held three times with the supervisor responding in a different way to the employee.

Roleplay One:

SUPERVISOR: Good morning, Sandy, how are you?
EMPLOYEE: I'm okay, except that I am having trouble with my project. I'm stuck and I don't know what to do.
SUPERVISOR: Don't worry about it. Let's just give the whole project to Sally. She'll know what to do.
EMPLOYEE: (looking despondent) Okay.

Roleplay Two:

SUPERVISOR: Good morning, Sandy, how are you?
EMPLOYEE: I'm okay, except that I am having trouble with my project. I'm stuck and I don't know what to do.
SUPERVISOR: Don't worry about it. I'll just take over myself. I know what to do.
EMPLOYEE: (looking despondent) Okay.

Roleplay Three:

SUPERVISOR: Good morning, Sandy, how are you?
EMPLOYEE: I'm okay, except that I am having trouble with my project. I'm stuck and I don't know what to do.
SUPERVISOR: Would it help to talk about it?
EMPLOYEE: Yes, it would.
SUPERVISOR: Tell me more about what is going on.
EMPLOYEE: Well, I keep trying to get the attention of the other team members to set up a meeting and they do not respond to my messages.
SUPERVISOR: How is that making you stuck?
EMPLOYEE: I can't move forward until I get a decision from these people on the issue that only they can answer before we move on.
SUPERVISOR: Sounds frustrating and important that you get an answer from these people. What have you tried to do to get their attention?
EMPLOYEE: I have sent two emails copying all members of the team and no one responds.
SUPERVISOR: What else can you try?
EMPLOYEE: I guess I can call them on the phone.
SUPERVISOR: What else?

EMPLOYEE: I can go to their desks.

SUPERVISOR: What else do you need to move forward with your project?

EMPLOYEE: Once I have the answer I need, I will just need to dedicate some time to complete the report, but it is too noisy and busy here in the office.

SUPERVISOR: What do you need to create that time and space?

EMPLOYEE: I could block out the morning, turn off my emails, and put on my headphones and just write.

SUPERVISOR: How can I support you?

EMPLOYEE: I am good with this plan. Thank you for helping me think it through.

SUPERVISOR: Let me know how it goes and if there is anything else I can do to help.

Following this roleplay, the facilitator asks the participants, "What was different in the approaches the supervisor took?" This activity gets the participants to immediately see the value of a supervisor spending a little time in a coach-like conversation. Note that the actual conversation in the roleplay tends to differ but the intent remains the same.

Early in the class, the students participate in an activity that allows them to explore the differences between mentoring, coaching, and providing direct feedback as a supervisor. The course continues the first day with the neuroscience about coaching and why it works. There is a focus on the three levels of listening and the students get to experience an activity where they listen for three minutes to a partner without uttering a word in response. The participants learn about the role of questions in getting your partner to "say more." The course introduced a coaching model to use with coaching conversations. The model is similar to typical coaching models. Demonstrations are given by the facilitators of the course of how the model can be used and followed in a coach-like conversation in the workplace.

As the course moves into the second day, more information about how people behave in the workplace is brought into the conversation. Concepts are borrowed from psychology and the science of motivation theory.

The participants are given the opportunity to practice coach-like conversations in pairs and are given gentle feedback and encouragement from volunteer certified coaches who are brought in to support the course. The facilitator emphasizes that the participants are not learning to be certified coaches. They are learning a model to follow when they and a direct report or peer decide that having a "thought partner" to think things through on something would be helpful. This kind of conversation could occur once every couple of months. By the end of the second day, the course moves into having casual and formal conversations in the workplace using more coach-like skills. The students are taken through a series of practices where they consider the topic and what about it can be coach-like versus more mentoring or more direct feedback. The list of conversations is:

- Welcoming someone new to the team
- Working with someone who need help
- Working on an Individual Development Plan (IDP)
- Talking with someone who is burned out and is considering leaving the organization
- Giving someone feedback on performance
- Helping someone who has received bad news (perhaps was not promoted)
- Engaging someone who is demonstrating misconduct

Through practice, the participants experiment with using a coach-like approach in many of these conversations, but also recognizing that the coach-like approach may not be sufficient in some cases.

The participants leave the course with the skills and confidence to use coach-like skills in the workplace. Some of them decide they want to learn more about becoming a professional coach, but for others, this training is enough.

Peer Coaching

Peer Coaching can be taught and practiced within an organization to enable partnerships among peers as they address workplace goals and issues together. Like Coaching Skills for Leaders, it is not a coach certification program and can be easily taught internally by facilitators of learning. L. Feingold, one of our coach pioneers, shared "As powerful as one on one is when you do the pure coaching, if people are looking for a culture shift and a performance shift, [peer coaching] creates culture and performance. So, I think you can't really have a coaching program without peer coaching.... you want to create a collective mindset, that's why it's so important, it changes culture quicker and is more inclusive." She also found adopting the peer coaching methodology for team meetings promoted the coaching culture as well as making the meetings more productive.

L. Feingold talked about Peer Coaching groups, usually consisting of five to six, that have a process they follow. The process can be introduced by a facilitator who transfers facilitation to the group once the group is comfortable. While L. Feingold has had success with peer coaching in both the private and public sectors, she talked about having more success offering a two-day class prior to the peer sessions for government employees and felt this worked better for this audience. The two-day experiential class taught coaching basics such as listening, asking questions, the power of the pause, and being comfortable with silence; but more importantly, it reviewed mindset and assumptions—it really was "an inside out" approach. The first day was learning and the second day was all coaching practice. If participants wanted to keep going after the initial training, they then joined a smaller group to continue peer coaching practice.

Dr. T. Fitzsimmons developed a three-hour training program on Peer Coaching that she gave to groups both inside and outside of her organization. The approach of the program is to provide a simple coaching model and allows the participants to practice providing peer coaching to each other. This short program emphasizes the importance of the agreement between the peers, the process itself, and the "rules" of the conversation.

The three-hour program is focused on individuals in the workplace who want to have a peer coaching relationship to help each other in some way. The training includes information on what peer coaching is and isn't. It provides training on the basic skills of listening and asking powerful questions. It also provides a model for the coach-like conversation, and guidance and emphasis on the agreement. In addition, training can include more specific coaching skills that would help the conversation move forward like validating, acknowledging, and using metaphors.

The agreement: It is important that when engaging in a peer coaching relationship that an agreement is established between the participants. Peer coaching is not a casual conversation between friends. It is a structured process with rules of engagement. The agreement should reflect the commitment to the process and be documented in an email or some other written format and should include at a minimum:

- The rules of how the conversations occur
- The goals for the peer coaching relationship or experience
- A statement about the confidentiality of the conversation
- Rules about how to handle if one wants to end the relationship
- A promise of accountability
- A promise to be reliable and meet at the agreed upon times.

The Process: How the peers are matched can be done in different ways. In this model, only two persons are matched, although many peer coaching groups include five to six participants. There may be an organizational reason for a pairing. Assuming that the peer coaching program is voluntary, the first order of events is to identify a peer with whom you feel confident you can have a reciprocal coaching relationship. Perhaps this is someone you already work with and know in the organization. Perhaps you face similar workplace challenges.

After identifying the match, peers need to meet to establish expectations. The rules of the engagement are discussed and the basic agreements such as the ones mentioned above are agreed upon.

At each session, someone is the coach, and the other is the recipient of coaching, commonly referred to as "the client." The client brings the agenda or topic for the peer-coaching discussion. It is the "coach's" role to listen and ask open-ended questions, following the coach-like model. The coach helps the client explore thoughts and options. The focus is on what action(s) the client can take into the future. The session ends with a commitment on what action the client will take.

The peers can set up their relationship as they see fit. They could meet daily, weekly, monthly, or other. They could agree on how long they meet each time, and if they want to take turns in the same session or alternating sessions.

While the peer coaching groups can be pulled together to support a topic brought in by its members as described above, L. Feingold introduced several useful and innovative variations. For example, L. Feingold facilitated a peer coaching program called *Mastering Contemporary Leadership Challenges: A Peer Coaching Cohort for Emerging and Senior Leaders*. In this peer coaching, the facilitator brings cutting-edge leadership concepts to the session that set the stage and participants solve real challenges in real time with peer support. For each meeting, the five to six participants would first read the leadership concept in advance and review a coaching skill. Practice included coaching skills and dialogue around the leadership concept. The seventh and last session was the integration of learning which allowed participants to reflect on what they were taking away. She found the common take away was that a change in their own "lens" or perspective had the greatest impact on their leadership. She felt providing a "safe place" to explore brought about self-awareness which was powerful to the participants. L. Feingold recommends interviewing everyone beforehand to discover what they want out of the program so you can adapt to their needs. In addition, providing a safe space is essential for participants to bring about self-awareness.

It should be acknowledged that since L. Feingold's Peer Coaching Cohorts required smaller groups and were labor intensive, it was important to obtain high-level stakeholder buy-in. L. Feingold leveraged the early participants to become the leaders and spokespersons for future groups. She also collected testimonials. One participant was recognized as the "Best Supervisor" with the "highest productivity for a team" in the organization and attributed her success directly to the program. Another shared that while he joined as a skeptic, by the end, he learned so much and felt that "if you don't continue this program, it's a tragedy." In addition, it does provide an opportunity to build the coaching culture that many leaders are trying to create. Based on these learnings, L. Feingold shared that she wished she had obtained more support to have more groups launched at once so there would have been a bigger impact across the agency and government more quickly.

Index

Printed in the United States
by Baker & Taylor Publisher Services